LIVING PROOF
Telling Your Story
to Make a Difference

Praise for

Living Proof: Telling Your Story to Make a Difference

"If we're going to make change, we're going to have to tell our stories and tell them effectively. This book shows us how."
Paul Loeb, author of *Soul of a Citizen*

"Everyone's talking about the power of stories these days but we need more resources to help advocates, activists and nonprofit communicators find their own voices, get heard and win real change. *Living Proof* is a sourcebook for trainers and advocates alike that fills that need. It's full of hands-on exercises, good ideas and useful suggestions."
Gordon Mayer, National People's Action

"The principles of rhetoric are translated here into contemporary language to make them accessible to anyone who wants to persuade through storytelling. This book provides instructions, examples, and exercises to make your stories come alive. A superb guide."
Dr. Sonja K. Foss, University of Colorado Denver, author of *Contemporary Perspectives on Rhetoric* and *Inviting Transformation: Presentational Speaking for a Changing World*

"This is an extraordinarily effective guide for advocates seeking all kinds of social and institutional change. But don't mistake it for another 'how to.' Above all, this book helps us to see how to take our lives seriously enough to tell them. The practices recommended in this book are a gift. A great read for all interested in what their stories can do for others."
Dr. Della Pollock, The University of North Carolina at Chapel Hill, author of *Telling Bodies Performing Birth* and editor of *Remembering: Oral History Performance*

"Stories have the power to bind us together, to bridge our differences, to build community. Sometimes the difference between hope and despair is a well-crafted story delivered with passion and focus. Now more than ever, our world needs ordinary people to become master storytellers. This book shows you how."

Eboo Patel, founder and president, Interfaith Youth Core and author of *Acts of Faith: The Story of an American Muslim, the Struggle for the Soul of a Generation*

"This book belongs on the shelf of every advocate and activist. *Living Proof* is a practical guide for getting your message heard by anchoring the message in the truth of your own experience. If you're working to change the world and need help with your story—read this book."

Michael Margolis, president, Get Storied and author of *Believe Me: a Storytelling Manifesto for Change-Makers and Innovators*

"We understand the world through stories. This book will help you understand why that is and how to take advantage of them to make the planet a better place."

Bill McKibben, founder, 350.org

"It's critical for the public to hear and be moved by the stories of injured service members and their families. *Living Proof* is a great tool for anyone sharing a story and hoping to move—and motivate—an audience."

Lee Woodruff, co-founder of the Bob Woodruff Foundation and author of *In An Instant*

"This book has been a useful tool for my staff and board. *Living Proof* has significantly shifted how we tell our story, and we've seen the result in how our community engages with us."

Susan Raffo, executive director, PFund Foundation

"Any person who needs to tell a story will benefit from reading this book and doing the exercises. I can't imagine any readers for whom this would not be true."

Leslie Shore, author of *Listening to Succeed*

"*Living Proof* is unique in its ability to inspire and empower advocates to ethically craft stories of their lives as instruments for social justice. I am so excited for my students to work with this book."

Dr. Tami Spry, St. Cloud State University, author of *Body, Paper, Stage*

"I have never read a more practical guide to advocacy. This book should be on every library director, trustee and advocate's desk for easy reference. I have already used some tips from the book during a press interaction. There's a natural fit between the content of this clearly written and useful book and the work of library advocates."

Michael Colford, director of library services, Boston Public Library

"This is like no other advocacy primer I have laid my hands on in the last 25 years."

Dr. Melissa L. Ness, MSW, president, Connections Unlimited

John Capecci and Timothy Cage

Living PROOF

Telling Your Story to Make a Difference

Essential Skills for Advocates and Spokespersons

Granville Circle
— P R E S S —

Published by
Granville Circle Press
2811 University Ave. SE #14445
Minneapolis, MN 55414
www.granvillecirclepress.com

Printed in the United States of America and
distributed by Itasca Books www.itascabooks.com
1-800-901-3480

Quantity sales. Special discounts are available on quantity purchases by nonprofits, corporations, associations and others. For details, contact the distributor at orders@itascabooks.com.

Orders for textbook and course adoption. Contact the distributor at orders@itascabooks.com.

Excerpt from *Soul of a Citizen* by Paul Loeb. Copyright 1999, 2010 by Paul Loeb. Reprinted by permission of the author.

Excerpt from *The Story of Your Life* by Tristine Rainer. Copyright 1998 by Tristine Rainer. Reprinted by permission of the author.

Excerpt from *Body, Paper, Stage* by Tami Spry. Copyright 2011 by Tami Spry. Reprinted by permission of the author.

This Granville Circle Press book is printed on paper that contains 50% post-consumer fiber with FSC certification, manufactured using biogas energy. Printers are powered by energy harnessed on the wind farms of southwestern Minnesota.

ISBN: 978-0-9838703-0-2
Second Printing

Library of Congress Cataloging-in-Publication Data
Capecci, John.
Living proof : telling your story to make a difference : essential skills for advocates and spokespersons / John Capecci and Timothy Cage.
Minneapolis, MN : Granville Circle Press, c2012.
p. cm.
1. Public speaking—Handbooks, manuals, etc. 2. Social advocacy—Handbooks, manuals, etc. 3. Social justice—Handbooks, manuals, etc. 4. Nonprofit organizations—Public relations.
I. Cage, Timothy. II. Title.
PN4129.15 .C34 2012   808.51
Library of Congress Control Number: 2011942125

Cover, interior design and illustrations—Brad Norr, www.bradnorrdesign.com
Indexer—Chris Dodge
Photos, page 193—Jim Tittle, www.nicepix.biz

DEDICATION

To all who do good things with their stories,
and in memory of those whose stories continue to inspire us:

Gianna Capecci
Deborah Voss Mankiewicz
Annie Lewis Martin

Contents

Introduction

Everybody likes ice cream, right?
That's the bet Ocean Robbins made as he stood before an audience of five hundred and told his story.

My grandfather started Baskin-Robbins ice cream company. Thirty-one flavors. (Audience applauds.) And from his earliest childhood, my dad, John Robbins, was groomed to one day join his father in the family company. He grew up with an ice cream cone-shaped swimming pool in the backyard and a commercial freezer in the garage, full of thirty-one flavors of ice cream at all times. He grew up working in the factory and he was expected to join the family business. But then, when he was in his early 20s, he was offered that chance and he said "no." And my grandfather was pretty hurt and said "Why? What has come over you?" And my dad said, "You know, dad, we live in a world under a nuclear shadow. Every two seconds another child is dying of hunger and malnutrition. The environment's deteriorating rapidly under the impact of human activity. And given those circumstances…
I don't think inventing a thirty-second flavor is an adequate response for my life.

Ocean delivered this keynote address at the National Alliance for Peace conference in Washington, DC. A tireless advocate for young people building a better world, he drew upon his experience to talk

1

about citizen responsibility and youth empowerment. He hooked the audience with his unique family history. And he told his personal story naturally and passionately.

While writing *Living Proof*, we've been fortunate to meet many people like Ocean who've found they can make a real difference telling their personal stories. Working for more than twenty years as communication trainers, we've helped thousands reach that same goal. Some, like Ocean, tell their stories on a national stage; many more share their stories in community meetings or with bloggers and local newspaper reporters. They're "ordinary" people and first-time speakers. They're also skilled presenters and media personalities. They speak in support of large and small nonprofits, local and national groups and publicity campaigns for the arts, the environment, education, health and youth. They stand at lecterns, sit in circles and knock on doors. They're interviewed over the phone and on-camera. They've appeared in high school gymnasiums, at the White House and on *Oprah*. But no matter where they're from or how much (or how little) experience they have, these people share the same objective: to tell a personal story with clarity, passion and purpose, and to have that story make a difference for someone or some cause. They are advocates.

In Roman law, the *advocatus* was called to plead others' cases in a court of justice. Today our use of the word *advocate* has expanded beyond the legal sense to include anyone working to make the world a healthier, safer and more just place. We wrote *Living Proof* for these many people because we've seen how, with the right support and coaching, ordinary people can become extraordinary advocates.

Personal stories have a unique ability to affect audiences. But it's not by story alone that successful advocates convince others to take action, whether that action is donating money, improving public policy or changing behavior. Advocating with story takes a specific kind of preparation. It requires practice with elements of persuasion, public speaking, media interview skills and storytelling—not to mention healthy doses of fortitude and commitment.

We also wrote *Living Proof* to provide advocates with a single resource for this special kind of preparation—a one-stop shop that gathers together what you need in order to stand up next week and tell your story effectively at a town meeting or on national television. We knew from experience that such a book didn't exist. When participants in our workshops have asked for additional resources, we could point them only to the many excellent works on storytelling, personal narratives, public speaking, media skills, persuasion, autobiography, civic action and citizenship. There was no single, accessible guidebook that pulled together the essentials and specifically focused on how to tell a personal story in this unique context—as an advocate.

Living Proof is based on our experience training advocates and draws from the work of experts and colleagues in many fields. It focuses on the essentials: what you need to know to tell your story effectively in public (from talks to keynotes) and media interviews (from blogs to broadcast). At the center are the **Five Qualities of Effective Advocacy Stories**. These qualities form a simple, strong foundation for success, wherever and whenever you tell your story. You'll find the Five Qualities echoed throughout *Living Proof.*

Preparation to tell a personal story publicly rarely follows a straightforward, linear path. It requires giving over to the fluid creative process—that back and forth, push and pull that happens as you craft your experience into story, adapt to changing settings and audiences, and manage your identity as a public advocate. That said, *Living Proof* does follow a general sequence—from the exploration of the power of stories, to ways of finding, crafting and preparing your story, to the specific skills needed to deliver powerful presentations and give great media interviews. You can certainly work through *Living Proof* from start to finish—over a weekend, a week or in conjunction with a course of study. You can also flip to the sections most useful to you right now or keep the book on hand as a resource. As with our workshops, we've tried to make *Living Proof* adaptable to individual needs.

- Each chapter title page previews what's inside.
- *Exercises* help you explore and plan.
- *Practice Runs* guide your run-throughs for specific speaking engagements or interviews.
- *Tips and Tools* offer advice on public speaking and media skills.
- *Prep Sheets* provide blank forms to use as you plan to give a talk or interview. Download additional *Prep Sheets* at www.livingproofadvocacy.com.

Throughout *Living Proof* you'll meet advocates from diverse walks of life. Many have generously shared their stories and experiences of being an advocate, and we're indebted to them for the richness they bring to this work. You can read more about them and view videos of their advocacy at www.livingproofadvocacy.com.

Advocates frequently describe the experience of "going public" as a combination of great uncertainty and incredible potential—what psychologists and anthropologists might refer to as a *liminal* experience: betwixt and between. Paul Loeb, in *Soul of a Citizen*, captures this sense of standing at the threshold of social involvement—and the rewards that come with stepping forward:

Rarely does social involvement place us in the path of destructive natural forces or armed opponents, but it does involve risk. At the very least, it requires us to make ourselves psychologically vulnerable. It impels us to overcome distracting habits and petty concerns, to challenge internal fears, and to face criticism from those who call our efforts fruitless, foolish, or a waste of scarce time.

In return, social involvement converts us from detached spectators into active participants. We develop new competencies and strengths. We form strong bonds with coworkers of courage and vision. Our lives become charged with purpose (34).

Your story *can* make a difference. We offer *Living Proof* as a guide. Advocate for the people and causes important to you, employing the single most powerful tool only you have—your personal story.

John and Tim

Get Ready

H owever you enter *Living Proof*—whether you read it from start to finish or flip to the sections that are most relevant to you—be sure to take these important steps.

- **Complete the two main exercises:** *My Six-Word Reason* **and** *Story Map*. *My Six-Word Reason* (page 20) is a great starting point, focusing immediately on your goals. *Story Map* (page 34) is the important foundation for much of the work in *Living Proof* and you'll return to it often.

- **Start speaking now.** While you may share your story in written form via blogs, websites or editorials, *Living Proof* is about the power of the *spoken* story. So speak out early and often. When you talk out your ideas, even stand and speak them, you train your body and voice, and this goes a long way in helping you become comfortable and confident on a stage or in a studio. Of course, there are times when you need to work things out on paper. But don't rely too heavily on the written word. Get used to speaking your work and you'll get ever closer to a comfortable and genuine telling.

- **Practice** *free-telling*. One way to get in the habit of speaking your work is to use *free-telling*, a composition technique based on *free-writing*. Free-writing is a stream-of-consciousness exercise used by writers to generate material and break through writer's block: the writer sets an amount of time (say five or ten minutes) and doesn't stop writing until the time is up. Not all of what is written is useable, but the exercise forces the writer to put on paper whatever comes to mind—often, great ideas that were lurking just under the surface. The principle behind free-telling is the same, and a number of exercises in *Living Proof* use this technique. Free-telling is particularly helpful as you search for the parts of your experience that will become your story, as you craft your language and as you practice for presentations and interviews.

> ### How To Free-Tell
>
> • Find a comfortable, private space.
>
> • Set a timer for two minutes.
>
> • Begin speaking and continue until the time is up. Don't critique yourself or worry that your story is coming out sloppily; free-telling is the verbal equivalent of writing a first draft or doodling. If you get stuck, just repeat the last thing you've said until a new thought comes to mind.
>
> • If you need to pause and jot down a moment of brilliance, do. But continue speaking immediately. If you're able to record your free-telling, listen for ideas or language you may want to keep in subsequent "drafts."

• **Decide how you'll capture your ideas.** Plan now for how you'll keep notes or record your insights from the exercises in *Living Proof*: a written or electronic journal, an actual or online filing system, a digital audio or video recorder.

• **Enlist partners.** Stories need listeners and speakers need audiences. As you work on your story, it will often take someone saying, "Hey, that's really interesting," or "I'm confused. Tell me more about that" or "Is that detail really necessary?" If you want to measure how your story takes shape or affects others, you'll need a partner or coach. A partner may be another advocate working on the same goals, someone from the organization you're working with or a professional communication coach. Regardless of who you choose, make sure it's someone who can provide candid and helpful feedback.

Working with a Partner

Be specific about what you'd like your partner to listen or watch for. Ask open-ended questions that prompt specific responses rather than questions that will get a yes or no answer. You'll get more useful information from "What part of my story can you visualize most clearly?" than from "So, was that okay?"

Chapter One

Your Story
as Living Proof

IN CHAPTER ONE

❏ How Advocates and Organizations Use Stories
❏ Why and When Stories Work—and Why and When They Don't
❏ An Important Exercise: *My Six-Word Reason*
❏ The Five Qualities of Effective Advocacy Stories

Answering the Call

*During a small fundraising event for a cancer-support
organization in Minneapolis, Derek Cotton stands in a board
member's living room, clutching a half-page of notes. He tells
guests what it felt like to be diagnosed with colon cancer and how,
when he lived in Texas, the Dallas affiliate of the organization
provided support that "...balanced me out. Kept me off the ledge."*

*Sitting with other parents in the library of her son's Brooklyn
grade school, Theresa Greenleaf calmly tells them what it's like
being the mom of a kid with food allergies, how appreciative she
is of the school's support and assistance—and how critical parents'
cooperation is to safeguarding all kids at the school with allergies
or asthma.*

*Loren Vaillancourt takes a deep breath as the news anchor of
CBS' The Early Show says, "You believe it was distracted driving
that led to your brother's death. He was just twenty-one years old.
What happened in that accident?"*

Every day, millions of people go public.

They stand up at community meetings to address their
friends and neighbors. They sit under bright lights in a television
studio, waiting for the interviewer's next question. They approach
lecterns, adjust microphones and look out at unfamiliar faces.

At rallies and fundraisers, in radio and television studios, in community
centers, on the phone with local reporters and in front of web cameras,
millions of individuals like you come forward daily to tell their stories.

They speak to raise awareness. They speak to change minds. They speak to educate, mobilize, give voice to under- or misrepresented people, promote a beneficial product or service and raise money. They speak for causes local and global—from creating safer schools to reducing the incidence of heart disease, from encouraging arts funding to ending homelessness. They tell their stories with anger, humor, hope, candor and passion. They go public with their personal and sometimes intimate stories not for their own celebrity—though they may, in fact, be celebrities—nor purely for dramatic effect—though their stories often are dramatic.

They tell their stories because they believe they can help others and make a difference.

Like you, they are advocates.

Whether you call yourself a spokesperson, activist, representative, change-maker or champion, if you speak out on behalf of someone or some cause, you are an advocate. Advocates fight for the rights of others. Advocates publicly endorse valuable products or services. Advocates raise

> The Latin root of *advocate* is *vocare* (to call), closely related to *vox* (voice).

funds for a cause. In each instance, the action at the heart of advocacy remains the same: speaking out. You are answering the call to help others and—in the true spirit of advocacy—are being vocal about it.

You may have come to advocacy on your own, it may be part of your job or you may have been asked to "put a face" on a campaign by serving as its spokesperson. You may be part of a large advocacy group or acting as a one-person crusader. However you've reached this point, though, you share an objective: to have your story move audiences from apathy to empathy to action.

When Derek Cotton told the people gathered in that Minneapolis living room of the support he received from Gilda's Club in Dallas, he was living proof of the value of this national cancer support organization. He advocated for opening a Gilda's Club affiliate in the Twin Cities, his new home. He spoke in support of others dealing with cancer, and he wanted the people in that living room to open their wallets.

When Theresa Greenleaf described to other parents the night her son suffered a severe allergic reaction and collapsed in the cab on the way to the hospital, she was living proof of the importance of vigilance. She advocated for compliance with school policies regarding allergens in packed lunches. She spoke in support of her son and others at the school. She wanted the parents in that school library to open their hearts.

When Loren Vaillancourt told the CBS anchor that her brother Kelson was killed in a traffic accident involving a distracted driver, she was living proof of the personal loss that results from a preventable accident. She spoke on behalf of others at risk on the road, and wanted viewers to change their driving behaviors and open their eyes.

Like Derek, Theresa and Loren, you are an advocate because you too hope your story can move others to act.

Why Stories Work

There are more than 1.5 million nonprofit organizations in the United States, and the vast majority relies on people like you to share stories and help them deliver their messages. Commercial businesses too depend on stories that will prove the value of their product or service, whether it's a vaccine that saves lives or a light bulb that saves energy. And every day, individuals committed to making a difference in their corners of the world are standing up to say, "Let me tell you what happened. Let me show you what I've seen."

What these diverse groups and individuals have in common is the belief that stories can provide compelling answers to the question: "Why should anyone care?"

Every day we see examples of how one person's story *can* make us care, inspire us or persuade us to act. A news feature shows an athlete overcoming personal challenges to win Olympic gold, and we re-evaluate our own goals and motivations. A beloved celebrity talks candidly about his battle with Parkinson's disease and, thinking of friends similarly affected, we make a donation. A bereaved mother stands up at a local school board meeting and tells how her son, the victim of a hate crime, complained

> Google™ "share your story" and you'll get millions of responses including the Kansas City Public Library, the Native American Advocacy Program, the Human Rights Campaign, the National Council of La Raza, the National Breast Cancer Foundation, the American Bible Society, Harvard University, Greenpeace and the Alaska Tobacco Control Alliance. The organizations and causes that rely on people like you to share a story are numerous and diverse.

about being bullied in the hallways, and we change our minds about how safe and inclusive our schools are.

The questions of how and why we respond to personal stories this way constitutes a vast field of study, spanning anthropology, psychology, theater, communication and folklore, as well as public relations, advertising and marketing. The power of storytelling is not news.

But some claim we are currently in a "golden age" of story, with storytelling skills encouraged in MBA and medical training programs, scientific institutions and law schools. The shelves of our local and online bookstores overflow with guides on how to tell stories to enhance our leadership skills, build community, alter our life's direction, leave an oral or written personal history for our families, brand our business and sell more widgets. All these applications are grounded in the same fundamental truth: we are storytelling beings. And when we use our own stories as tools for advocacy, we tap into an essential and universal quality.

The ability to see our lives as stories and share those stories with others is at the core of what it means to be human. We use stories to order and make sense of our lives, to define who we are, even to construct our realities: this happened, then this happened, then this. I was, I am, I will be. We recount our dreams, narrate our days and organize our memories into stories we tell others and ourselves. So, as natural-born storytellers, we respond to others' stories because they are deeply, intimately familiar.

But story also speaks to us differently than other types of communication. If you've ever sat through a mind-numbing "data-dump" presentation in which a speaker bombards you with statistics and diagrams, you've experienced the hunger for story. Through tears of boredom, you wish with all your heart the speaker would step away from the PowerPoint® of bar graphs and pie charts, look at you and say, "Let me give you an example of what I mean. On my way to the lecture today…" Ah, you'd prick up your ears, suddenly on familiar turf. Abstract ideas become concrete. Knowledge is colored with emotion. Not a world of generalities, but one of specific sights, feelings, drama, dialogue and people.

When the stories you tell are from your life, you give audiences an opportunity to feel and imagine with you, to understand in a meaningful way just why they *should* care. The enormity of problems like hunger and social injustice can certainly motivate us to act. We can be convinced logically of the need for intervention and change. But it is the story of one individual that ultimately makes the difference—by offering living proof.

When Derek Cotton was asked by Gilda's Club Twin Cities to speak on behalf of the organization and to share what he had experienced at the Dallas Gilda's Club affiliate, he had never told his cancer story publicly. He says, "When I was asked to tell my story, my first response was, 'I don't think I'm your guy. I don't have this fantastic story to tell. I don't have anything dramatic to say.' I had cancer. I got better." But the organization knew Derek had an important experience to share with their potential donors. Gilda's Club was raising funds to open a "clubhouse" in the Twin Cities. There wasn't yet a building they could point to and say, "This it is. This is what happens here. Support *this*."

The Universal Need for Connection

A recent study at the Wharton School asked participants to read three stories and contribute $5 to alleviate hunger in Africa. In one version, their donation would go to a particular seven-year-old girl in Mali named Rokia; in the second, to millions of suffering Africans; in the third, to Rokia—but in this version, she was presented within the larger context of world hunger: "Rokia is just one of millions suffering from hunger." The study found that people were more likely to give directly to the story of Rokia—not to anonymous millions and not to Rokia when presented as part of a larger scenario. Stories of individuals draw upon our universal need for connection.

But Derek had attended a Gilda's Club when he lived in Dallas. He knew what happened there, what it looked like, what it felt like, even how it smelled. The Gilda's Club Twin Cities affiliate needed him to tell *that* story. So at a one-hour fundraising breakfast attended by four hundred people, he helped the audience "imagine a place" where people living with cancer could receive emotional and social support outside the sterile hospital walls.

It felt like I was going into someone's house. Right off the bat, when you walk in—"I'm not in a church basement, it doesn't smell like a hospital, I'm not in a little room with bare walls that's very clinical." I didn't feel like I had to walk in and say, "Hello. My name is Derek Cotton and I have cancer." It's a totally different feeling. You walk into a Gilda's Club and you're in a home. And after a while, it sort of becomes your second home.

The first time I went, a very cheery woman met me at the door and said, "Hi, how are you? Let's go chat." So we go to this little room and it was like sitting in someone's den. I told her "I don't know why I'm here. I have cancer and I don't know what I'm looking for. I'm just lost."

She said, "We can handle that." And she showed me around.

They had cooking classes to better your diet, art, music, all sorts of different activities every day of the week. Even stuff for my boys: kids' night, games, movies, popcorn. There was a potluck every month. Sometimes, I'd just go there in the afternoon to do my work. I felt comfortable there. It was a place to go where my boys and I were understood, where we felt like regular people. I actually felt like I could get away from my cancer at Gilda's Club.

I was surprised when I moved to Minneapolis and there wasn't a Gilda's Club. The Mayo Clinic is near here, there are major health corporations headquartered here. It's a big city. I just assumed there would be one.

Derek's story touched people at the breakfast fundraiser—many of whom knew intimately the emotional and psychological needs of someone dealing with cancer. In that one hour, with Derek's help, the organization raised nearly $500,000 toward its capital campaign. He made a difference for Gilda's Club Twin Cities.

What difference did Theresa and Loren's advocacy make? After hearing Theresa's story and a talk by an allergist, parents at the Brooklyn grade school fully cooperated with new school policies regarding allergens packed in school lunches. Loren, an advocate for stricter "distracted driving" laws, gets emails from young people who pledge to stop texting while driving. She says the emails reading "Thank you so much, you totally changed my mind" keep her going and enable her to tell the difficult story of her brother's death.

What keeps you going? What *will* keep you going? Use the following exercise to find out.

EXERCISE

MY SIX-WORD REASON

Objective: *Explain—briefly—how you got here and why you're an advocate.*

Use this exercise to:
- Claim your identity as an advocate, if you're just starting out
- Refocus your story, if you're already speaking as an advocate
- Pinpoint the reason you're telling your story
- Find concise, effective language
- Generate headlines and hooks

How short can a story be? Frederic Brown is credited with the shortest horror story: "The last man on Earth sat alone in a room. There was a knock at the door." Ernest Hemingway was once purportedly dared to write a story in six words. He penned, "For sale: baby shoes, never worn." In 2006, the online storytelling magazine SMITH (www.smithmag.net) asked writers to summarize their lives in six words. The Six-Word Memoir® project spawned a popular book series that includes "terse true tales" of the human experience such as:

Joined Army. Came out. Got booted.—Johan Baumeister
Learning disability, MIT. Never give up.—Joe Keselman

My Six-Word Reason is our spin on the Hemingway and SMITH challenges. We use it to jumpstart our advocacy workshops. Rather than trying to capture an entire life story in six words, this exercise focuses on **your personal reason for being an advocate.**

The exercise:
- Imagine someone asks you, "*Why* are you an advocate for this cause or organization?"

- How do you answer—**in six words?** Not five words, not seven. Six.

MY SIX-WORD REASON *(continued)*

Here are a few examples:

An art mentor changed my life.
> Jamal, a board member for an organization that pairs artists with disadvantaged youth

I was deaf, now I hear.
> Carol, recipient of a cochlear implant and an advocate for hearing loss issues

I've seen too many hungry children.
> Roberta, an advocate for ending world hunger

> *"I love life, justice and humanity."*
> **Ocean Robbins**
>
> *"Son's near death brought new life."*
> **Theresa Greenleaf**
>
> *"Gilda's Club gave me a home."*
> **Derek Cotton**

Some important guidelines:

- This is a *personal reason,* not a goal. *I've seen too many hungry children,* not *I want to end world hunger.*
- Use your six words however you'd like. Your reason may be a full sentence or two three-word phrases.
- Your reason might capture the one moment that drove you to be an advocate, an entire lifetime or a core belief.
- Don't worry about finding *the* right six words. Generate as many reasons as you'd like.
- Give yourself time. Keep track of your work. Save your reasons and return to them later. You'll definitely end up using one or two when you speak.

_____ _____ _____ _____ _____ _____

_____ _____ _____ _____ _____ _____

_____ _____ _____ _____ _____ _____

_____ _____ _____ _____ _____ _____

When Stories Work

T hink of a time when you were moved *and* motivated by someone's story. Not *just* moved—to laughter, to anger, to joy or compassion—but actually motivated to *do* something. You listened to the story and then signed on the dotted line. You picked up the phone. You reconsidered your actions, rethought a belief or repeated the story to someone else. What was it about the story that made you take action?

Chances are it wasn't the story alone that made an impact.

Here's the secret truth successful advocates and the organizations that rely on them know: as much as we believe absolutely in the power of story to engage and move audiences, advocating well with personal stories is not a call to simply "Insert Story Here." A story alone—or an advocate who's not suitably prepared—can miss the mark. But with attention to five particular qualities, the effective advocacy story is within anyone's reach. Before we look at those five qualities, let's consider what might lead to a less-than-successful advocacy story.

Generally, there are two types of stories that can fall short: the *raw* and the *canned*. When you hear a **raw story**, you might perceive the advocate as nervous, fragile, unfocused or out of control. He or she may ramble on too long or seem overly frank. Often, your response to a raw story is to feel *for* the advocate, rather than connect *with* the advocate. A **canned story**, by comparison, feels overly prepared: it appears slick, detached, scripted. You know a canned story when you hear one. It's when your first response is, "He's told that story a lot," or even, "She's really good at this." Stories you perceive as either raw or canned distract you from the advocate's purpose and focus you instead on the advocate himself or herself. A raw story may make you worry about the advocate's emotional state; a canned story may make you skeptical of the advocate's intent.

While no one *intentionally* aims to present a story as raw or canned, new advocates often have impulses that can lead—unintentionally, but understandably—to raw or canned presentations and interviews.

I Want to Keep It Real. New advocates sometimes say, "I don't want to lose the emotion or the freshness of telling my story, so I'll just wing it." While you should always bring genuine emotion and passion to your speaking, to rely solely on this is risky. Why? Because without preparation, winging it may result in a raw story—unfocused and unstructured. Speaking off-the-cuff and from the gut may be completely appropriate in other instances, but as an advocate it can place you in an emotionally vulnerable spot, doing disservice to your story and your cause. With media interviews, especially, lack of preparation means you'll be at the reporter's mercy. But there are ways to be both genuine *and* prepared.

I Want My Story to Be Memorable. We once sat in a room with an inspiring group of women advocates for WomenHeart: The National Coalition for Women with Heart Disease. All had suffered some form of cardiovascular trouble—congenital heart disease, heart failure or multiple heart attacks. Their stories were amazing. Every one of them provided living proof of why we need to pay attention to heart disease in women. Each shared her story, and when it was Helene's turn, she began, "Well, my story isn't very dramatic. I only had the one heart attack."

There is no competition among stories. Your story doesn't have to be extraordinarily shocking to be memorable and have an impact. True, the events of one life may seem more sensational than another, but this doesn't discount individual experience. The power of your story may not lie in its drama, but in its absolutely perfect relationship to your cause. When new advocates like Helene feel their experiences "aren't very dramatic," it can cause them to remain silent. In other cases, it can lead to a canned story.

When new advocates feel their personal stories aren't dramatic enough, they may push to the *melo*dramatic, embellishing the theatrical, turning their stories into canned products that are ready for YouTube's "Most Viewed." Maybe it's because we're fed a media diet of SHOCKING TRUE STORIES. It's true, reporters—who naturally think in terms of powerful stories—are often first attracted to drama. And while it is helpful to have a hook to your story, if you ramp up the drama artificially, you can lose the heart of the telling and the simple sincerity. But there are ways to be both engaging *and* forthright.

I Want to Speak Out, but the Thought of Speaking in Public... Any type of public speaking can be intimidating; sharing a personal story only increases the anxiety, and may cause you to either under-prepare (raw) or over-prepare (canned). You've probably heard that public speaking is one of humankind's greatest fears, and that most people dread it more than death. Every year, it seems, another public opinion poll supports this attitude. Ask people to name their top fears and public speaking will rank among the top five. It's clear that

Public Speaking Fears through the Years

A recent survey of Top Ten Fears places public speaking alongside "terrorism" and "financial ruin." In the 1980s, it competed with "nuclear destruction." In the 1970s, "shark attack."

putting yourself in the spotlight can be an anxiety-ridden activity—without preparation and practice, that is. People often feel the same about media interviews, fearing that all reporters are either "out to get them" or won't understand the point. Actually, what reporters really want is a good story, told well.

The nervousness people feel going into any public presentation can keep them from adequately preparing, and result in them showing up raw. Ironically, nervousness can also lead to a canned presentation or interview. We once coached a woman preparing to tell her story for the first time. It dealt, tragically, with the loss of two of her family members in two separate drunk driving accidents. Preparing for a coaching session, she emailed us a script, saying, "This is what I plan to read." We noted immediately that she had written her story in the third person: "When she was 12, her mother died in a car crash and the little girl couldn't understand how this could happen." In the final sentence, she revealed, "I was that little girl." While this may have been a dramatic approach to her story, our conversations revealed the real reason she had written it this way: She was terrified she wouldn't be able to control her emotions in the act of telling. Removing herself from the story and reading it word for word was a way of protecting herself emotionally. The result, however, might have come across as a recited, canned presentation. After some coaching, she decided to tell the story in the first person and gave a more heartfelt, if somewhat less polished, telling. There are ways to be both confident *and* extemporaneous.

Between the raw and canned extremes, you'll find the perfect balance for sharing your personal stories as an advocate: neither under- nor over-prepared, neither fragile nor distanced, media-ready and not at a reporter's mercy. The effective advocacy story is crafted, confident and flexible. It's authentic and focused on the audience and message, enabling listeners to empathize so you not only move them, but also motivate them to act.

THE RAW STORY	THE EFFECTIVE ADVOCACY STORY	THE CANNED STORY
Underprepared	Practiced	Over-rehearsed
Emotionally fragile	Emotionally engaging	Emotionally distanced
Unstructured	Crafted	Slick, polished
Nervous	Present	Detached
Impromptu	Improvisational	Scripted
Unfocused	Flexible	Rigid
Vulnerable	Authentic	Distanced
At mercy of the media	Media-ready	Sensationalized
Focused on advocate	Focused on audience	Focused on effect
Unrestrained	Genuine	Insincere
Audience feels bad for speaker	Audience connects with speaker	Audience analyzes speaker

The Five Qualities of Effective Advocacy Stories

To strike the right balance between raw and canned stories, bear these five qualities in mind each time you advocate with a personal story. These are the hallmarks of a well-told advocacy story. We'll explore these qualities throughout *Living Proof*, but here's a quick introduction.

1. Advocacy Stories Are Focused. Telling a personal story to a loved one late at night differs from sharing with a therapist, which differs from telling it at a party. In each situation, the reason for telling your story changes, and while you may not always think about *why* you tell your stories, there *is* intent. Telling your personal story as an advocate demands that you be explicit in your intent. The more tightly you link your story to your goals and messages, the more successful your advocacy.

> *"I was advocating for parents of kids with severe allergies. I was also advocating for my son, Jack. I needed other parents to know that the safety of all children is of paramount importance, that their cooperation is necessary and appreciated."*
>
> **Theresa Greenleaf, about speaking to other school parents about awareness of food allergies**

2. Advocacy Stories Are Positively Charged. Every successful advocacy story is about change, and that change happens to you. The change may be large or small, dramatic or subtle, a seismic upheaval or a slight shift. But there *is* a change in you. And that change is positively charged. Whatever your story and its particular theme, when used as a tool for advocacy, it will point to some positive change. A positive change your story shows is needed, a positive change your story shows is possible.

> *"How do I tell my story in a way that leaves the listener hearing a positive message of triumph rather than a story of victimization? I do not want to be seen as a victim or have people feel sorry for me. I want them to see people have value."*
> **Becky Blanton, advocate for the homeless**

3. Advocacy Stories Are Crafted. While all of us are born storytellers, we may not all be *practiced* storytellers. Sharing your personal story as an advocate requires you to explore and practice some fundamentals of storytelling. Those fundamentals include arranging and revising, choosing and polishing language. And—one of the most useful skills you can develop as you prepare your story, especially for media interviews—editing.

> *"People love when I mention the ice cream cone-shaped swimming pool my dad grew up with; how he learned that 'blood is thicker than ice cream.' Once you find a good phrase that makes people smile, keep it."*
> **Ocean Robbins, peace and environmental advocate, grandson of Baskin-Robbins ice cream company founder**

4. Advocacy Stories Are Framed. For your story to stand as compelling living proof, it cannot stand alone. It must be framed, indicating the particular way you'd like audiences to view or understand it and its importance, what it is and what it is not. Framing can mean the difference between a story perceived as heartfelt and genuine, and one seen as whining, self-serving or preachy. Framing refers to the things you say that help your audience receive your story as you intend.

> *"It is not a plea for sympathy. It's about what we can learn from this."*
> **Loren Vaillancourt, on telling the story of losing her brother in a traffic accident involving a distracted driver**

5. Advocacy Stories Are Practiced. Somewhere between the raw and the canned is the style of speaking that is effective in most situations, one that features your natural speaking style, is genuine and confident. But being natural, genuine and confident takes practice.

> *"I practice. I practice and practice ad nauseam. And the story will change a little bit and the messages will change a little bit—but I've learned to go with the flow."*
> **Kathy Kastan, heart health advocate**

Effective advocacy stories are:

Focused

Positively Charged

Crafted

Framed

Practiced

Map Your Experience

IN CHAPTER TWO

- ❑ How to Find the Raw Material for Your Story
- ❑ An Important Exercise: *Story Map*
- ❑ How to Treat Your Experiences Like an Old Shoe

Explore the Entire Landscape

B ecky Blanton is a journalist who, at times, has been homeless. The last time was following the death of her father, when she spent 18 months living in a 1975 Chevy van parked at a Walmart. Telling the story, she says:

> *I don't know when or how it happened, but the speed at which I went from being a talented writer and journalist to being a homeless woman, living in a van, took my breath away. I hadn't changed. My I.Q. hadn't dropped. My talent, my integrity, my values, everything about me remained the same. But I had changed somehow. I spiraled deeper and deeper into a depression.*

Then a friend found Becky and told her that an essay she had written about her father a year before had been selected for the book *Wisdom of Our Fathers: Lessons and Letters from Daughters and Sons.* The editor was the late Tim Russert, then host of NBC's *Meet the Press.* On tour to promote the book, Russert talked enthusiastically about Becky's writing. The irony of this—that her work was being noted in the national media while she lived in a parked van—struck Becky deeply and marked the beginning of her emotional recovery, her return to work and the eventual end of her homelessness.

Of course, there's more to the story than that. There were the periods of couch-surfing, managing her cat and Rottweiler, dealing with summer heat and winter cold—and what Becky learned about societal attitudes toward the homeless.

A year later, Becky was given a six-minute opportunity to tell her story publicly for the first time. She needed to decide what—of this deeply personal and complex experience—would be best to tell for the benefit of others.

It took a week of wrestling with the story to come up with the speech I did. I lay in the back of the van (I still drive it) and put myself back in time to relive parts of the experience. I had to drill down to the raw emotions of the experience and convey in six minutes what I'd learned and experienced in eighteen months. I asked friends who had recently learned of my situation what they wanted to know. I took that into account.

When you ask someone "Will you tell me your story?" what have you really asked? Are you asking them to begin from their earliest memory, walk you briskly through the awkward teen years, detail their adult milestones, then describe the eggs they had for breakfast, say how their day's been and end with whatever thoughts they had circling just before you asked, "Will you tell me your story?"

Probably not. Few people have that kind of recall and few listeners that kind of patience. But when you were first asked to tell your story as an advocate, or when you first considered sharing your story, the landscape may have seemed just as vast: Where do I begin? How much do I tell? What *is* my story?

Don't get paralyzed feeling that you must find the *right* story, the *one* story you tell whenever you speak or give an interview. There are many ways to tell your story. Each time you do, you select bits of your experience and arrange them differently. While you may sometimes have the chance to give a long interview or a keynote address that allows you to relate your experience in detail, you will most often tell short stories. In the case of media interviews, *very* short stories.

The first step in deciding what to tell and how to tell it is to explore everything you have available as story material. Author Shirley Jackson, writing in *Experience and Fiction*, suggests a way to approach life to find the story: "attack it in the beginning the way a puppy attacks an old shoe. Shake it, snarl at it, sneak up on it from various angles" (199).

Use the following exercise, the *Story Map*, to shake and snarl at the whole of your experience: everything you've seen, heard, said and felt that urged you to speak out. Obviously, no one can access and recount all those experiences, and you won't bring everything you remember with you each time you speak. Not everything will be relevant or safe or appropriate to disclose. But this is where you start.

EXERCISE

STORY MAP

Objective: Create a visual map of your experience.

Use this exercise to:
- Explore the entire landscape of your experience
- Recall the details of your experience
- Find the potential for vivid and engaging living proof
- Create a visual reference you can return to again and again
- Find other stories you may have overlooked

For this exercise, you'll construct a visual map of the experiences that led you to be an advocate. If that sounds like a huge investment of time or if you don't consider yourself a gifted visual artist, relax. You can give as little or as much time to this as you'd like: sketch it out quickly in preparation for an upcoming talk or make it the basis of an elaborate and ongoing journal of your experience. Either way, it's

---

STORY MAP *(continued)*

important to find out what you've got to work with. *Story Map* asks you to be expansive, to generate as much material as you can, much more than you could possibly use—a story so big and full of detail that you'd never be able to tell it at once.

Why start here? Because memory fails us. Because you may find the story you thought you should tell is not the one you end up telling—or, at least, not the only one.

The exercise:

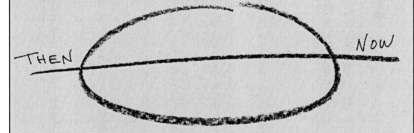

- **Use whatever media is comfortable and at hand.** Use a pencil and paper, a pen and the back of a napkin, marker and whiteboard, sticky notes on the wall or a computer application. Have your note-taking method with you to record ideas that come up while creating the *Story Map*.

- **Draw an elongated oval.** Imagine you've drawn it around the whole bundle of experiences that made you want to speak out. Within this oval there may be a lifetime of events or perhaps only a period of your life.

- **Draw a horizontal line** through the center of your oval, with the ends of the line extending beyond the oval.

- **Label the area to the left of the oval** *Then* **and the area to the right as** *Now*. *Then* represents you before your journey to become an advocate. *Now* is you as an advocate. The line connecting them is your timeline of events: this happened, then this happened, then this.

STORY MAP *(continued)*

- **Mark and label events and moments on the timeline with X's or dots.** Begin with the obvious: most of our experiences center around a key incident, a crisis or a revelation. But don't forget the small moments. At this point, nothing is unimportant. Get it all in there.

- **Populate your map.** Stories are about people. Who was with you at various points in this experience? Who did you see and to whom did you speak? Who was watching you? Who left you a voicemail or sent you a text? Locate and label those people with X's or dots.

That's the basic structure of the *Story Map*—the universe of your experience, the moments that occurred and the people involved (the setting, the plot and the characters).

Some important guidelines:
- How detailed and elaborate you make your map is up to you.
- As you fill in the map, it may help to pull out a photo album or two, or look back at a calendar.
- If you're a writer, a journal-keeper or an artist, look to some of your other autobiographical work.
- Talk with the friends, family members, colleagues and others who shared your experiences.
- You'll return to the map a number of times, so make multiple copies.

Find and Focus Your Story

IN CHAPTER THREE

❏ How to Decide What to Tell, What Not to Tell
❏ Getting Clear on Your Goals, Audience and Key Messages
❏ Thinking Like a Film Director, an Archaeologist or a Quilter

Choose What to Tell

F inding your story begins with trying to remember how things happened, what was going on and who was there. You plot it out (using the *Story Map*) to catch the fragments that may have fallen through the cracks of memory and time. This process of recalling experience is ongoing and different for everyone.

But telling a story is not just reciting life events as they occurred. It's the selection of moments, arranged in creative ways, that makes a story. Before doing that, all we have is experience.

To find the story in your experience, you have to decide which parts to select and arrange. "The ability to find story in your life depends upon cutting it into pieces, and the nature of the stories you find depends on how you slice them," writes autobiographer Tristine Rainier in *The Story of Your Life* (47).

Take another look at your *Story Map*. Imagine literally slicing it up by drawing vertical lines at various points.

Advocacy Stories Are Focused

When you tell a personal story, you tell it for a reason. You may share a story with a loved one to bond or explain yourself. You may tell your story to a therapist to make sense of a behavior or to heal. You may tell stories at parties to entertain or commiserate with friends. When you speak as an advocate, your reason needs to be clear so that your audience understands why they should consider your goals or mission—that is, what you are proving. Advocacy stories are focused, determined by explicit goals, for particular audiences, with specific messages.

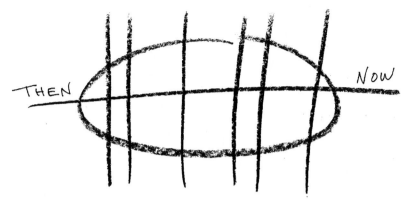

There are countless ways you might do this, taking a moment from here, an image from there, an insight from one day and a snippet of conversation from another. You might cut a wide swath from the center or thin slivers from either end. But you can't tell your whole experience. So how do you choose?

If your experience is one that is emotionally charged, you may choose what to tell by answering the questions: "How personal or candid should I be?" and "How personal or candid am I comfortable being?" Your answers depend on many things, such as how close you are to the experience—both psychologically and in time—and how often you've spoken about it. Your answers may also depend on how the people closest to you might react to what you have to say. Decisions about personal disclosure are different for everyone.

> "When an experience takes root in our lives, it often grows up into a story."
> **John Elder, _The Story Handbook_**
>
> "All memories are not stories. Cooking up egg foo yung is not a story."
> **Roger Schank, _Tell Me a Story_**

The Five Qualities of Effective Advocacy Stories help you navigate this terrain. For example, Loren Vaillancourt, an advocate for distracted driving laws, points to the importance of _focus_ and _practice_ when telling the difficult story of her brother's death in an auto accident:

Telling my brother's story and saying what happened, it's really emotionally overwhelming. I was not able to get through my story at first. There was no way. It took practice. I had to talk it through to myself. I had to take a moment, find a way to get myself out and realize what's important. It's about being able to ask, "What is the point of this story?" And honestly, if you practice it, it helps you with that [emotional] transition: "I'm trying to get my point across here so, okay, where do I need to go next?"

> *"You will know when it is time to tell the story, you will also know when it is not time. Some experiences need more gestation time than others. Listen to yourself."*
> **Tami Spry, *Body, Paper, Stage***

If the emotional content of your experience is something you're considering as you choose what to tell, keep these tips in mind.

- **Know your boundaries, but don't omit the heart.** Sometimes you have to step outside yourself to look at your story objectively. At other times, you have to dive deeply into it. Your goal is not to distance yourself from emotions or to bare your soul in the name of full disclosure. Your aim is a balanced and effective story— neither raw nor canned—that is emotionally engaging, not fragile or distanced.

- **You are the author of your experience.** The decision to disclose or not is *always* yours. Never leave that decision to chance or to others—for instance, to a reporter or audience member who asks an inappropriately personal question.

- **Remember your goal and your audience.** Ask: what is required of this moment, this audience, at this event or interview? What you decide to share may be appropriate for some audiences but inappropriate for others. Knowing your audience is key. Some audiences will require bold and graphic honesty, while others may require a gentler, more measured approach.

Use the following exercise, *What Makes the Cut?* to look at your *Story Map* from a number of different perspectives and to find potential story elements.

EXERCISE

WHAT MAKES THE CUT?

Objective: Compile potential story elements.

Use this exercise to:
- Find bits of experience to shape into stories
- Uncover the relationship you have with your story
- Change the perspective on your experience; step outside yourself
- See how versions of your story may come together differently

How your story takes shape depends on how you slice your experience. And you've got many ways of deciding what makes the cut. If the analogy of slicing and cutting is too rough, film makers, writers, folklorists and artists offer plenty of others. *What Makes the Cut?* is an exercise with five variations to explore these analogies. Each asks you to view your experience from a different perspective. Try each variation and give each some time.

The exercise:
- Grab your *Story Map* and some sticky notes. Use the notes to label areas of your map. You could also make multiple copies of your map and mark them up.

- Keep a list of the moments revealed by each of these variations.

WHAT MAKES THE CUT? *(continued)*

Variation #1: Life as a Movie

Think of your *Story Map* as the raw material for a bio-pic like *Gandhi*, *Patton* or *What's Love Got to Do With It?* Just as a screenwriter selects scenes to tell the main character's story (gentle Gandhi, prickly Patton, triumphant Tina Turner), choose elements from your experience to tell your story.

Some labels to apply:
- Great Opening Shot
- The Realization
- Climax of the Story
- My Enemy
- My Hero
- Funny Moments
- Victory Moment
- Great Closing Shot

Variation #2: Life Snapshots

If you had photos of all the moments in your *Story Map*, which would go into an album of your story?

Some labels to apply:
- Five Best Shots
- The One Shot That Captures It All
- My Favorite Shot

Variation #3: Secret Stash

There may be moments from your *Story Map* you'd prefer to keep locked away as not ready for public presentation. What are the moments on your map that you remove?

Some labels to apply:
- Maybe Someday
- If It's Needed
- My Secret

WHAT MAKES THE CUT? *(continued)*

Variation #4: The History

Imagine your map is an archaeological timeline like *The Evolution of Dinosaurs* or *A Timeline of Ancient Greece*. How do events on your map fall into periods or eras?

Some labels to apply:

- Geographic Locations
- Time Periods
- Happy Times
- Hard Times

Variation #5: Life's Fabric

The metaphor of fabric arts (stitching, weaving, quilting) is perhaps one of the most common in describing story-making. If you were sewing together your experience into a story, how would you choose the swatches?

Some labels to apply:

- Similar Patterns
- Rough Times
- Smooth Times
- Harmony
- Contrast
- Intricate Weavings

Focus on Your Goals and Audience

Before trying to answer, "*What* is my story?" ask "*What am I trying to do* with my story?" Knowing your goals makes it easier to choose what to tell and to focus your story. It also gives *you* focus.

You have both general and specific goals to reach with your story. **General goals** are long-term results of your advocacy. General goals name the better world you imagine, the difference you ultimately want to make: "To create a healthier planet" or "To change attitudes about homelessness." You won't reach a general goal with one speech, one interview or one story. But you can definitely help get there. **Specific goals**, on the other hand, are what you hope to achieve at the time you speak: "To move the people at this fundraiser to fill out their donation cards" or "To get people to march with us" or "To have listeners call their doctors to discuss their risk factors."

"Be very, very, very clear about your motives and your goals. When you know what you want to do with your story you'll know if you've achieved it. I want people who hear my story to reconsider what it means to be homeless. I want my story to spark conversations. I want it to change the way people see each other and themselves. I want it to inspire people. I want to make people feel like they aren't the only ones going through tough times—because they aren't."
Becky Blanton, advocate for the homeless

Just as you have general and specific goals, you have general and specific audiences. Your **general audiences** are those broadly defined groups of people you hope to reach. You probably had a general audience in mind when you first decided to go public: "People who care about saving the planet" or "Other parents." Your **specific audiences** are the actual, living, breathing people you speak to: the crowd that hears you at the rally or the commuters who listen to your radio interview. Effective advocacy stories are

To get a complete picture of the specific audience for your next talk or interview, see *Being Audience-Centered* (p. 91) and *Know Your Target Audience* (p. 110).

focused on audience, just as they're focused on goals.

Use the following exercise to explore how aiming for your specific goals and audience can help you focus and shape your story.

EXERCISE

LINK TO YOUR GOALS AND AUDIENCE

Objective: Let your specific goals and audience shape your story.

Use this exercise to:
- Be clear about what you want to achieve
- Think like your audience
- Find bits of experience to shape into focused stories

Imagine having the attention of thousands of people. Heck, tens of thousands. Aim high: You're standing on the steps of the Lincoln Memorial. Or you're giving a television interview on a major network. Or a popular

Use this exercise with *The Better World* and *What You Need to Know,* the *Practice Runs* on pages 131 and 132.

talk show host does a special cause-related segment and features you as the guest. Who do you most hope is watching that show? Who would benefit most from hearing your story? What do you want them to do or understand?

The exercise:
- **List the specific audiences you have in mind** in the left-hand column of the table on page 46.

LINK TO YOUR GOALS AND AUDIENCE *(continued)*

- **List your specific goals** in the center column of the chart. They may be your personal goals or the goals of the organization you represent.

- **Return to your *Story Map*** and use it to help fill in the right-hand column. For each audience and goal you've listed, look for the moments in your *Story Map* that show the goal is important.

Audience	My Goals	Moments That Show Why The Goal Is Important
High school kids	*To make them understand the impact of losing a sibling to a senseless accident*	*The morning I woke up and realized I had become an only child*
Women in my audience	*To make them understand the importance of paying attention to their bodies*	*How I had not paid attention to my own symptoms for eight months*

Focus on Key Messages

eart health advocate Kathy Kastan went from being an "eager but anxious" first-time speaker to a national spokeswoman. The main advice she now gives to other advocates is on the mark.

Your story is important, yes. Your story is significant, yes. But the most important thing, if you want to make a difference, is to focus on why it's important to the people you're talking to. Get to those key messages.

Key messages say what you want your audience to act upon or learn. Key messages help decide what story you tell and what parts you emphasize. For speeches, key messages determine how you structure your content. For media interviews, they're the main points you'll cover, regardless of how an interview proceeds. Effective advocacy stories are focused on key messages.

How do you know what messages are key messages? Think: "If nothing else, I want my audience to understand *this* after hearing my story." Key messages are the minimal requirements for what you communicate. You want audience members to repeat your key messages to others. You want journalists and reporters to highlight those messages in their stories. Strong key messages form the backbone of your presentation or media interview.

Here are some guidelines for composing good key messages.

- **Key messages are full sentences.** "Our streets should be safe for our children" is a good key message. "Safety" is not a key message, it's a bullet point.

- **Key messages are statements.** "The first step is to contact our congresspersons" is a good key message. "What's our first step?" is not a key message, it's a question.

- **Key messages are concise and specific.** "Water is everything" is a crisp, clear key message. A paragraph outlining the social and political importance of clean drinking water is not a key message, it's a treatise.

> Scott Harrison, founder of **charity: water**, uses the key message "Water is everything" to focus his stories on the organization's mission: bringing clean and safe drinking water to people in developing nations.

- **Key messages are memorable.** "Music can literally make your soul *pop* and move your spirit to a higher and better place," is a key message people will remember. "Empowering young people to affect global change beginning in their local communities by utilizing holistic development and pre-professional programs in creative entrepreneurship" is a mission statement.

> When Glenton Davis, founder of Soul Pop University, used this key message ("Music can literally make your soul *pop*.") in a media interview for *Trends* newspaper, he practically handed the writer the headline: "Nonprofit Organization Makes Music 'Pop' for Students."

- **Key messages should be limited to three points—five at the most.** If you try to cover seven important messages in a presentation, the audience will have trouble remembering and prioritizing them. In a media interview, it's doubtful you'll have time to hit all seven. Even if you do, some may be edited out.

If you serve as an advocate for a particular organization, you may have key messages handed to you. If they're not, read the organization's printed materials or visit its website to find its messages and explore how your story can support them.

Because key messages are important to so many aspects of your advocacy success—focusing your story, structuring your speech, keeping an interview on track—you should have them with you at all times. Post them in your workspace. Carry them in your wallet. Refer to them often as a way of staying focused and on message.

Use the next exercises to write memorable key messages and link them to your story.

EXERCISE

COMPOSE KEY MESSAGES

Objective: Write three key messages that are to the point and memorable.

Use this exercise to:
- Be clear in your intent and message
- Craft language

You'll find that the time spent polishing rough ideas into concise and memorable key messages is well worth it. The clearer your key messages are to you, the clearer they'll be to your audience.

The exercise:
- **Craft three key messages** that meet the criteria. Think: "If nothing else, this is what I want my audience to understand or do."

COMPOSE KEY MESSAGES *(continued)*

Key Message #1

_____

Is it a full sentence?
Is it a statement?
Is it concise and specific?
Is it memorable?

Key Message #2

_____

Is it a full sentence?
Is it a statement?
Is it concise and specific?
Is it memorable?

Key Message #3

_____

Is it a full sentence?
Is it a statement?
Is it concise and specific?
Is it memorable?

LINK TO KEY MESSAGES

Objective: *Let your story stand as living proof of your key messages.*

Use this exercise to:
- Focus your story on your key messages
- Find parts of your story that are the strongest for your advocacy goals
- See how different key messages can change your story

How you tell your story and what you tell may change depending on your messages. Use this exercise to determine which parts of your story best support and illustrate your key messages.

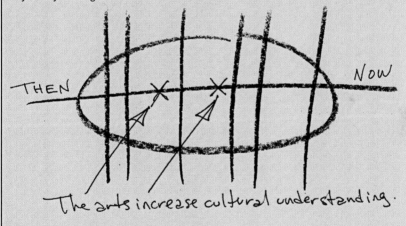

The exercise:
- **Return to your** *Story Map.*

- **Write a key message below your map.** This could be one of the messages you wrote in the previous exercise or it could be a message provided by your sponsoring organization.

Use this with the exercise on page 71, *Look Here*, to practice articulating the links between your story and key messages.

LINK TO KEY MESSAGES *(continued)*

- **Draw lines** that connect your message to specific moments in your *Story Map*. Ask:

    What moments from my story connect most powerfully to that message?

    What moments provide the best example of this message or demonstrate its importance?

- **Repeat this exercise with your key messages** each time you prepare for a speech or media appearance. Key messages change; your story will too.

Name the Change

IN CHAPTER FOUR

Stories Are about Change

I messed up, but I made it right.
I was lost, now I'm found.
I stood idly by, now I must act.

In its simplest form, a story is a string of events happening to someone, somewhere. The most important part of that definition? "Happening to someone." Stories are about action, about movement, about *what happens to someone* as she or he moves from Point A to Point B to Point C. Typically, we refer to this as a story's plot; think of it more simply as the *change* that occurs.

From ignorance to insight: *I was blind, now I see.*

From one perspective to another: *I used to think that, now I think this.*

You might express the change as one of transformation: "I was X, then Y happened, now I'm Z." Change can be psychological, physical, literal or metaphorical. The change may even be that you have found the motivation to tell your story: *I was silent, but I am silent no more.*

Advocacy Stories Are Positively Charged

Every successful advocacy story is about change, and that change happens to you. When you tell your story as an advocate, that change is always positive. This doesn't mean that you only focus on the good and the happy or that you sanitize your experience. Far from it. You may have endured great hardship, seen injustices or suffered great loss. Or you may have enjoyed great successes, been inspired by others or garnered win after win. Regardless of the course your story follows, your main goal as an advocate is to speak on behalf of others and *make a difference*. And that difference is a positive one. Your story is living proof that positive change is needed, possible and perhaps even inevitable.

On the *Story Map* (page 34), you drew an oval and then filled it with the whole of experience that led you to speak out. Bracketing the oval are two words: *Then* and *Now*. Your story is the story of the changes that happened between *Then* and *Now*.

For example:

Then: Neither Kathy Kastan nor her physicians recognized the early signs of heart disease. She was ill and ill-informed.

Now: She is an authority on heart-healthy living and a national advocate for raising awareness of heart disease in women.

Changes: From innocence to knowledge. From illness to health. From passivity to action.

Then: Scott Harrison was a New York nightclub promoter living a fast, selfish and arrogant life, "chasing models and bottles."

Now: Founder of **charity: water**, he's dedicating his life to serving others, helping millions get access to clean drinking water.

> "My family story represents a journey from success defined as a life of unlimited consumption, to success defined as a life of unlimited compassion. It is the journey from the old American dream of business accomplishment to a deeper American dream of health and contribution."
> **Ocean Robbins, peace and environmental advocate**

Changes: From self-interest to compassion. From excess to access.

Then: Loren Vaillancourt was devastated by her brother's death in a car accident, and found herself suddenly an only child.

Now: She's seen how telling her story can make people stop talking and texting while driving.

Changes: From grief to hope. From mourning to motivation.

The change, the "something that happens," is what turns experience into story. Your audience will be listening for it. But if the change you point to is negative, your audience might dismiss your story as "just" confession, complaint or vent. It's important to name the positive change that has occurred in you. Naming the positive change also will help you

- decide which parts of your experience to share to communicate that change
- stay focused on your advocacy goals
- keep media interviews on track
- frame your story
- cast yourself in your story the way you want your audience to see you.

Naming the positive change also helps you double-check how ready you are to go public. If you find it difficult to name the positive change and are locked in anger, frustration, grief or pain, take time to think through your stance as an advocate and how you feel about it. If you can't name the positive change you're working toward, you may be setting yourself up to tell a raw story: emotionally fragile, vulnerable, at the mercy of the media.

> "My experience could have left me bitter, hostile and immobilized. But I knew that my heart couldn't stay in that dark place or it would destroy me and hurt my family."
> **Kathy Kastan,**
> **heart health advocate**

Here's an example. It's a transcript of a local television news story—with names changed—that captures an all-too-common situation in which an advocate with an unclear positive change inadvertently plays into the defeatist attitude set by reporters.

The news story is about an upcoming 3K run/walk to raise money for lung cancer research. The anchor introduces the story, then hands it off to a reporter conducting a live interview with a man who recently lost his wife to lung cancer. She left behind three children. This was devastating and shocking because the woman had never smoked a day in her life.

While the man is obviously committed to the cause, it's clear from his attitude that he's still distraught, having lost his wife only months ago. He manages to deliver some key messages at the end of the interview that point to positive change (more awareness of the disease, more funding for research), but the overall effect is neither hopeful nor motivating. Instead, the reporters' questions focus on the family's loss and feelings of helplessness. You see a grieving man, not an advocate pointing to the positive change made possible by the fundraiser.

On location at the local cancer center, the reporter asks the man, "Tell us about your wife." The man tells of the difficulty diagnosing the disease and realizing "there was nothing we could do."

REPORTER: Okay. What did you feel like when you first found out?

MAN: Well, it was a whirlwind of emotions. You really can't—I probably can't describe adequately what you feel, but, umm, disbelief, shock. You're sitting there enjoying somewhat of a normal family and then all of a sudden your wife—healthy, never smoked a day in her life—is being told she has lung cancer.

REPORTER: Mm-hmm.

MAN: And so that certainly goes against all the stereotypes you hear. But more importantly, when you, you know, get involved in the treatments here and you find out how many people do suffer from that devastating disease and just the sheer numbers. So, it hasn't been a journey of just one, there's a journey of many. But for us, it was just shocking to go through that.

REPORTER: Now, what is your part in the event coming this weekend, the fundraiser?

MAN: Well, she went through a series of aggressive treatments and to say that she was determined is probably an understatement. But even with the best treatments available, there were still— it wasn't enough to beat the battle, so...

REPORTER: Right.

MAN: So, I think, if anything, just to increase the awareness, hopefully empower people to want to be a part of organizations like this, because there's so many unmet needs in this devastating disease and certainly nobody deserves lung cancer. And so, if we can make people more aware of that and they can provide funding, important funding for treatments and resources and that's a wonderful thing and do good things.

Before tossing it back to the anchor, the reporter is compelled to mention: "You have three kids. One of them, Eric, is having a birthday today. Do you want to say happy birthday to him?" The man bravely manages a smile to the camera and a "happy birthday."

REPORTER TO ANCHOR: So, we're going to wrap things up from here. But, isn't this a horrible story Diane? It's so scary to hear this.

ANCHOR: Yeah, I mean it's one of those things where you ask yourself, "Okay, what can I do to protect myself?" And really the answer is not very much.

REPORTER: Nothing you can do for it.

ANCHOR: Yeah, which does not sit well with most of us.

Though the anchor closes with a quick mention of the upcoming run/walk, the somber tone has been set and that's where it stays. How could "naming the change" have helped this valuable advocate steer the interview toward his positive message while still honoring the emotional content of his story? Perhaps his change could be expressed this way:

Then: Stunned and shocked by losing his wife to lung cancer.
Now: Committed to telling others about this disease so this doesn't happen to others.
Changes: From devastation to dedication. From paralysis to power. From hurt to help.

With this change in mind, the interview might have gone like this (revisions in italics):

REPORTER: What did you feel like when you first found out?

MAN: Well, it was a whirlwind of emotions. You really can't—I probably can't describe adequately what you feel, but, umm, disbelief, shock. *There are a lot of people here at the Cancer Center who've been through that same shock and disbelief. It's horrible. That's why we're so*

59

motivated to come together to do something. We don't want others to have to live through this, and with more funding, better treatments and resources, we know we can make a difference.

REPORTER: You have three kids. One of them, Eric, is having a birthday today. Do you want to say Happy Birthday to him?

MAN: [to camera] Happy Birthday, Eric. [to reporter] *He'll also be joining us at this Saturday's 3K run/walk—he wouldn't miss it.*

> This is also a great example of how to reframe your story (Chapter Six: Frame It).

Here's another example of how naming the positive change helps. Becky Blanton, advocate for the homeless, first had the opportunity to tell her story at a TED Global Conference, a popular meeting of minds dedicated to "Ideas Worth Spreading." After telling the audience the story of how she found her way out of homelessness, Becky concluded her presentation by naming the change: "Three years ago I was living in a van in a Walmart parking lot. And today I'm speaking at TED. Hope always, always, finds a way."

Use the following exercise to name the positive change your story will convey.

NAME YOUR CHANGE

Objective: *Articulate what happened between Then and Now, ending in this positive act of advocacy.*

Use this exercise to:
- Decide what parts of your experience to emphasize
- Stay focused on your goals
- Keep media interviews on track
- Double-check how ready you are to go public

Earlier in this chapter, we summarized the positive changes expressed in stories told by advocates Kathy Kastan, Scott Harrison and Loren Vaillancourt. Using the same format, how would you name the story of your change?

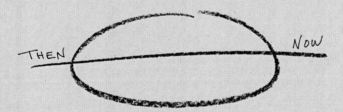

The exercise:
- **Look at your *Story Map*,** and especially at the words bracketing your experience: *Then* and *Now.* Consider: *How are you different now than you were at the start? What do you know now that you didn't know before?*

- **Look again at the examples on page 55,** then fill in the blanks below. Step outside yourself and write it in the third person as someone looking at your story. Use *he* or *she* or refer to yourself by name.

NAME YOUR CHANGE (*continued*)

Write a sentence or phrase that describes you **Then.**		
Write a sentence or phrase that describes you **Now.**		
List words that describe the **change** or **changes.**	**From:**	**To:**
List words that describe the **change** or **changes.**	**From:**	**To:**
List words that describe the **change** or **changes.**	**From:**	**To:**
List words that describe the **change** or **changes.**	**From:**	**To:**
List words that describe the **change** or **changes.**	**From:**	**To:**

Chapter Five

Craft Your Story

IN CHAPTER FIVE

❑ Telling Short Stories, Long Stories and Everything in Between
❑ Finding the Language of Story
❑ Crafting the One Line (or Two) That Will Hook Your Listeners

From Experience to Story

You are a born storyteller. And you naturally craft your stories, though you may not always be conscious of doing so. But think of a funny story you've told a number of times. Or an episode from your childhood, a brush with greatness, your proudest achievement or a bad customer service incident you've told frequently. The thirtieth time you told that story was probably different from the first time. What changed? The first time you told it you may have been remembering as you went along. Telling it a few more times, you noticed your listeners' attention wandering, so you did some editing. Maybe you found you could hook listeners by starting with the "payoff"— "Did I ever tell you about getting kicked out of my senior prom?" Sometimes you told the story in great detail, other times you summarized it quickly.

It's this same level of craft you want to apply to your advocacy stories:

Advocacy Stories Are Crafted

There are great stories—and there are boring stories. There are stories that make an impact in just twenty words and those that are long-winded, take too many detours and lose the thread (or mix too many metaphors). Just because a story is personal, perhaps even dramatic, doesn't mean it's ready to go public. Advocacy stories need to be crafted with basic storytelling techniques.

Crafted Doesn't Mean Canned

New advocates sometimes worry that crafting will make their stories feel canned, over prepared, slick. But crafting doesn't mean turning stories into something they're not or pushing into melodrama. Crafting helps you aim for the balance between raw and canned.

decide how to assemble the parts of your experience, choose what stays in and what comes out. Adjust the pace to tell your story quickly or in great detail. Use the language of story, which is different from the language used for reporting data. Perform what storytelling and screenwriting guru Robert McKee calls "the creative conversion of life itself into a more powerful, clearer, more meaningful experience" (27).

Assemble the Flexible Story

Being able to scale your story for sound bites, keynote addresses and everything in between is one of the most useful skills you can learn as an advocate. Scaling enables you to sometimes summarize your entire *Story Map*, as when heart health advocate Kathy Kastan says:

> *I went to a doctor feeling strange. He misdiagnosed me, told me I'd be fine. Went jogging in high altitude, collapsed. The symptoms were more serious—came home, saw another doctor. Misdiagnosed again, then found a doctor who got it—but I ultimately needed bypass surgery. Now I'm good. That's my story in a nutshell.*

Read more of Kathy's story on page 101.

At other times, you may focus only on scenes, as U.S. Representative Tony Coelho did when he spoke to fellow legislators in support of the Americans with Disabilities Act. Seated at a microphone as he addressed political colleagues, he described being diagnosed with epilepsy:

> *I always remember very well what happened and that I walked to the doctor's office from my car, sat in the doctor's office, was told about my epilepsy, got back in my car and drove back to my fraternity house. And I was the same exact person—but only in my own mind. Because the world around me had changed.*

You tell a succinct story to a potential donor with whom you share an elevator or to the television reporter conducting a short on-camera interview. As a keynote speaker or in a longer interview, you have the luxury of more time and can go into more detail. To be ready for any speaking or interview situation, your story needs to be flexible, and flexibility comes first from how you assemble your story.

Here's an everyday example.

Let's say you're visiting a friend for the weekend and you haven't seen each other in a while. To reminisce and catch you up, your friend (apparently highly organized) takes out a stack of photo albums. She lays the albums out before you. "This one is all college pictures, this one is vacations..." She gives you a photographic tour of her life. She starts with Album #1, the oldest photos, and together you look at each picture, turning page after page, pausing occasionally to look more closely or to listen as your friend tells what else was happening around that moment. You finish Album #1 and move to Album #2. At Album #3, she says, "Y'know? This album is just vacation shots. We can come back to those later if you want to, but they're kind of boring ... Florida, Mexico, New York, Florida, Florida." and she skips to Album #4. You ask, "Hey, what ever happened to your cousin Byron? He was hilarious." She reaches for Album #5 and there's the adult Byron mugging for the camera at a barbecue last year. She grabs Album #2 and there's thirteen-year-old Byron with the same mug. There's Byron in college. There he is at six years old. Clearly, Byron is alive and well and as goofy as ever.

> "The first time I told my story was for an edited video piece and I wasn't sure what to say. I thought I had to say everything. 'This happened, then this happened, then this happened.' My descriptions of things were lengthy. The next time, speaking at a fundraiser, I had 7 minutes. At last week's event I had 3 minutes. So one of the things I've learned is that I can be just as effective in three minutes as I am in seven minutes—and still tell the same story."
> **Derek Cotton, advocate for cancer support services**

It's a simple analogy: assembling your life experiences into stories is like giving someone a photographic tour of your life. Sometimes you show *"how it happened."* Other times you say *"look here."*

Assembling Story #1: How it Happened

Just as your friend began her photo tour with Album #1, you may guide audiences through your story chronologically, pausing at times, sometimes skipping ahead, but keeping things moving forward. You tell *How it Happened*, walking your listeners along the timeline of your *Story Map*: this happened, then this happened, then this. Album #1, next page, next page. Album #2, next page, next page. This approach is useful when it's important for audiences to understand the order in which things occurred or the effects over time. Kathy Kastan's story, summarized on page 66, lists events in the order they happened, from the first doctor's visit to her bypass surgery and return to health.

Assembling Story #2: Look Here

Or you might choose to tell your story the way your friend responded to your question about cousin Byron, assembling bits and pieces in a random order. This approach gathers scenes into a collage, saying, "Look here. Now here." Chronology isn't important; *Look Here* relies on cumulative effect, so scenes may be out of order. Master storyteller Jack Maguire refers to this as the *portrait gallery* approach: Imagine the scenes of your experience framed and hanging on gallery walls or the walls of your home. You shine a flashlight to direct viewers to "look here. Now here. And now here." Because chronology isn't important, the *Look Here* approach lets you move backward then forward in time, selecting and narrating the moments you choose. This approach is useful for illustrating specific points, for example, offering three short scenes that show the importance of one big idea.

Speaking at the Big Omaha tech conference, Scott Harrison illustrated his key message that "water is everything" with stories of what he had witnessed in the water-deprived villages of Africa. Scott used the *Look Here* organization this way: he told of kids in northern Uganda who, instead of going to school, walked back and forth along the road, in the hot

Read more of Scott's story on page 104.

middle of the day, carrying forty-pound containers of water. Then he told of a woman near the border of Sudan, dipping a bucket into a mud hole saying, "This is the water I take home, like an animal, and give to my kids." Then to a girl in Ethiopia who, when she gets her period, stops going to school because there are no toilets. Accompanied by Scott's dramatic photographs, his presentation was a literal and vivid gallery of support for his key message: Water is everything.

Adjusting the Pace

Quick. Tell your story in one minute. Now thirty seconds. Now ten seconds.

No problem, right? Just talk faster, then faster still.

While speed-talking can certainly be a useful skill, it's not the most powerful way to engage your audience. The ability to be nimble and to scale your story—without turning it into a tongue-twister—lies in deciding where you spend your storytelling time.

To vary the rate and length of your story, get to know these basic storytelling tools: *scene*, *description* and *summary*. They're the narrative equivalents of hitting play, pause and fast forward on your streaming video or DVD.

• **Scene** Hit ▶ to tell your story as if it were happening—as when you and your friend took time to look at individual photos in sequence.

- **Description** Hit **||** to slow down or freeze your story—as when you and your friend stopped to look at a particular photograph and talk about it or when you left the photo and went off on a tangent.

- **Summary** Hit **▶▶** to zoom through your story—as when your friend condensed her vacations into "Florida, Mexico, New York, Florida, Florida."

Use the following exercise, *Right-Size Your Story*, to practice assembling your flexible story and adjusting its pace.

EXERCISE

RIGHT-SIZE YOUR STORY

Objective: Practice collapsing and expanding your story

Use this exercise to:
- Learn how to be brief and flexible

This is an exercise with five variations that ask you to assemble your story in different ways, then practice using scene, description and summary. Keep track of these long and short versions. You'll definitely use them in your advocacy work.

The exercise:
- **Grab your *Story Map* and a partner.** You could also free-tell and record yourself.

RIGHT-SIZE YOUR STORY *(continued)*

Variation #1: How It Happened
- Look at your *Story Map* and give yourself three minutes to summarize the whole thing, from *Then* to *Now*. Tell your story in chronological order, but decide what moments to include.
- Now give yourself two minutes.
- Now one.
- Now 30 seconds.

Variation #2: Look Here
- Choose one of your key messages (page 47).
- Look at your *Story Map* and select three scenes that relate to that one message.
- State the key message, then talk through the scene. Say how they relate.
- State the message again and talk through the next scene. Say how they relate.
- State the message again and talk through the next scene. Say how they relate.

> Use this variation with *Link to Key Messages* on page 51.

Variation #3: Summary
- Choose a large section of your timeline, one that covers a good amount of chronological territory.
- Summarize that section of time and tell what happened within it.

Variation #4: Description
- Focus on one moment and describe it in as much detail as you can.

Variation #5: Summary-Description-Summary
- Select one moment to describe in detail. Look at everything that happens before that moment and after it.
- Summarize what happens before, describe the moment in detail, then summarize what happens after.

The Language of Lived Experience

G ood stories transport listeners to other places and times. They bring to life scenes, characters and actions. To do this, stories require language that moves beyond the simple reporting of facts to the conjuring of sights and sounds, thoughts and emotions. When the stories you tell are your own, that creative language comes from your lived experience.

As an advocate, you bring something to your cause no one else can provide: your lived experience in all its messy humanness. This may sound obvious, but the reason a spoken story differs from a written story in its power to move an audience is that there is a speaking, breathing body present telling the story. Yours is the body that experienced this story and audiences respond to that—*if* you use language that originates in your lived experience, language that helps audiences understand what things looked, felt and sounded like. As autobiographic writer Tristine Rainer notes in *The Story of Your Life*, "Experience is all we have, and it is only through our bodies that we have it, and only through our senses that we can know and convey it" (211). To bring your story to life for audiences, follow these guidelines:

It Starts in the Body

As performer Tami Spry notes in *Body, Paper, Stage*, audience response to your lived experience is a bit like an episode of a television crime drama series like *CSI*:

"It starts with a body, in a place, and in a time. The investigators analyze the body for evidence, the body as evidence, the body of evidence."

- **Appeal to All the Senses.** Give your audience sensory details to make your story come to life: the look, the feel, the sound, the smell, even the taste of things. You don't need to make every moment excessively detailed. That could cause sensory overload. But look for opportunities to get specific when describing moments, objects and feelings.

> Look: *I noticed a fly on the boy's eyelid as he reached out his hand to me.*
>
> Feel: *When I stood in front of the sculpture for the first time, my knees went weak. I was light-headed.*
>
> Sound: *The oil bubbled up, popped, slurped—then nothing.*
>
> Smell: *The forest air smelled like cold mushrooms.*
>
> Taste: *I spoke to the doctor, the taste of the pill still in the back of my throat.*

- **Tell Both Outer and Inner Stories.** You can tell your story from the "outside," saying what happened on the surface: "I got back into my car and drove home." Or you can go "inside" to tell what you thought and felt: "I got back into my still-cool air-conditioned Volvo, thinking of the face of the child I had just seen. My hands were shaking." Sometimes it's necessary to remain on the outskirts of your story to summarize it quickly. But if you stay outside you won't give listeners a chance to understand the emotional or sensory content. If you stay inside your story you risk alienating audiences and drawing too much focus to yourself. The most effective storytellers move from outer to inner and back again.

> *"It was strange, because at the time—a lot of my friends didn't really know how to deal with me. Y'know: I had cancer. Everyone wants to empathize with you: 'Is there anything I can do?' and all that. When they'd say, 'I understand what you're going through ...,' I knew what they meant. I used to say the same thing to people. But when you're going through it, you realize, 'You know what? I didn't have a clue before what others were going through.'"*
>
> **Derek Cotton, advocate for cancer support services, spontaneously brings to life the people in his story, their words and his own inner voice**

- **Populate Your Story.** Stories are about people. While you are the main character (the protagonist), your story involves others. Look for opportunities to describe those populating your *Story Map*. Quote them. Tell what you said to them and to yourself. Include dialogue.

- **Make Creative Links.** Use analogies to help your audience make imaginative connections between your story and something else—something familiar to them or something they never would have considered. For example, heart health advocates often say the feeling of a heart attack is "like an elephant stepping on my chest." Advocates fighting a mighty opponent often refer to the biblical David vs. Goliath story—an important reminder that analogies and most figures of speech are culturally specific. Consider whether your audience will share the same references you do.

> *"Then, while jogging with my dog one morning, she pulled me into what I thought was just another illegal dump. There were weeds and piles of garbage and other stuff that I won't mention here, but she kept dragging me—and lo and behold, at the end of that lot was the river. I knew that this forgotten little street-end, abandoned like the dog that brought me there, was worth saving. And I knew it would grow to become the proud beginnings of the community-led revitalization of the new South Bronx. And just like my new dog, it was an idea that got bigger than I'd imagined."*
> **Majora Carter, sustainable development advocate working to "green the ghetto" of the South Bronx, compares the abandoned East River waterfront to her adopted dog**

Use the following exercise to practice finding creative and evocative language.

EXERCISE

MAKE LANGUAGE LIVE

Objective: Practice drawing creative language from your lived experience.

Use this exercise to:
- Find new ways to express your ideas and story moments
- Remember how you experienced your story
- Create "full-color portraits" for your listeners

Bringing evocative, creative language to personal storytelling takes time: time to remember what the experience was like for you. Time alone, in quiet reflection, then time with a partner to try out your language. Time to look in a thesaurus for just the right word.

This exercise has four variations.

The exercise:
- Grab your *Story Map* and a partner. You could also free-tell and record yourself.

Variation #1: Activating the Senses
- Choose a moment on your *Story Map*. Close your eyes and imagine being there: What do you see? Hear? Smell? Is there a particular taste in your mouth? What does your body feel?
- Describe that moment taking each sense in turn.

Variation #2: Staying Out, Going In
- Choose a moment on your *Story Map*.
- Think about the difference between what was happening on the surface and what was going on inside, in your mind and your body.
- Describe the "outer" then the "inner" story.

MAKE LANGUAGE LIVE (*continued*)

Variation #3: Populating Your World
- Look at your *Story Map* and the people in it. Choose one person.
- Describe the person physically.
- Describe the person's voice. What is he or she saying?
- Describe your relationship to that person.

Variation #4: Comparing/Contrasting
- Choose a moment on your *Story Map* that is particularly vivid for you.
- Compare the moment to something else: "It was like…"

Hooks and Headlines

A hook is a phrase that dangles before you and gets your attention, teases you, grabs you and takes hold—just like a fishhook.

"Two years ago, I died on the operating table."

"My grandfather started Baskin-Robbins ice cream company."

Like a coat hook, it's a place for you to mentally hang things, a reminder of the theme or importance of a story.

"I had proudly served a country that was not proud of me."

"I was the same exact person. But the world around me had changed."

Like the hook on a dress or a jacket, it fastens things, secures them in your mind so you repeat them to yourself and others.

"Cancer gave me membership to an elite club I'd rather not belong to."

"The containers they walk around with to carry water are the iPods of Africa. Every child has one."

And like a boxer's right hook, it can pack a wallop.

"We were told how much college would cost. I didn't realize it could cost me my son's life."

Hooks are ear-catching phrases that make you want to hear more or read on. They are so perfectly pithy, catchy and crisp that they may capture the essence of your entire story in just a few choice words. When you lead off with a hook, it becomes a headline. Hooks help your audience remember key content and the theme of your story. They make it easy for audience members to tell others what was memorable about your story. In interviews, your hook may provide the interviewer with the title of his article or the quote that accompanies your photograph. It may help editors select which clip to use from your television, radio or web interview.

Spend the time and challenge yourself to construct one, two or three really good hooks. For ideas, look at your *Six-Word Reason* (page 20), your goals (page 45), your positive change (page 61), your key messages (page 49) and the following exercise.

EXERCISE
HOOK YOUR AUDIENCE

Objective: Create ear-catching phrases

Use this exercise to:
- Find memorable phrases that summarize your experience
- Discover other ways to express a key message

They're called *hooks* and *headlines* for a reason. Next time you're online, take note of the banner ads and the news summaries at the top of a web page. When you

HOOK YOUR AUDIENCE (*continued*)

watch television, note the scrolling hooks at the bottom of the screen. Look at magazine cover stories while standing in the check-out line for inspiration in creating your own eye-catching, ear-pricking phrases.

The exercise:
- Here are five ideas for creating sparkling hooks. Feel free to base yours on the examples here.

1. Use a fact your audience may find intriguing or almost unbelievable.	
Two years ago, I died on the operating table. **Heart health advocate** *My grandfather started Baskin-Robbins ice cream company.* **Ocean Robbins, peace and environmental advocate**	**Try it:**

2. Repeat a key phrase to unify your story.	
I was the same person, but the world around me had changed… I hadn't changed as a person, the world around me had changed. **Rep. Tony Coelho, advocate for the Americans with Disabilities Act** *Even those symptoms didn't get my attention … the doctors weren't paying attention…pay attention and listen to your body.* **Kathy Kastan, heart health advocate**	**Try it:**

HOOK YOUR AUDIENCE (*continued*)

3. Use analogies to make direct or indirect comparisons.

	Try it:
Having ovarian cancer = "a club I'd rather not belong to." **Gilda Radner, comedian** *The forty-pound Jerry cans children in Africa use to transport water = "the iPods of Africa."* **Scott Harrison, advocate for clean drinking water**	

4. Juxtapose two contrasting ideas.

	Try it:
We were told how much college would cost. I didn't realize it could cost me my son's life. **Deb, advocate for the National Meningitis Association** *I had proudly served a country that was not proud of me.* **Eric Alva, advocate for equity in the military**	

5. Use humor and wit—*if* it's appropriate to the setting and topic, you know your audience and the humor comes naturally to you.

	Try it:
Help me make green the new black. Help me make sustainability sexy. **Majora Carter, advocate for environmental justice** *My father learned that blood is thicker than ice cream.* **Ocean Robbins, peace and environmental advocate (from the Baskin-Robbins ice cream family)**	

Frame It

IN CHAPTER SIX

❏ Making Sure Your Story Comes Across as You Want It To

❏ How to Respond When Your Story Is Misheard

Provide Perspective

The idea that a framework can affect how we respond to something, or whether we notice something, has proven useful in understanding how we communicate. The concept has been explored in linguistics, communication, sociology and political science and is based on a simple analogy: just as a picture frame asks us to focus on whatever it surrounds, each of us creates *mental* frames that shape the way we see the world. Those mental frames are our values and beliefs, and operate like the frames around pictures; our minds focus only on what we want to see within that mental frame, ignoring or at least giving less attention to what is outside the border.

> ### Advocacy Stories Are Framed
>
> Your beloved three-year-old niece or nephew draws a crayon masterpiece on a lunch bag. To display it, you could stick it on the refrigerator door with a magnet or place it in a modest black frame and add it to the family photo wall. Or… you might have it professionally framed: a museum-quality beveled matte under UV-protected glass, a blonde wood frame that is the perfect contrast to the child's wild use of Periwinkle and Burnt Sienna. Whatever display you choose will say something to viewers: *"Isn't this cute?"* or *"This is not a scribble. This is serious artistic talent."* Like the crayon drawing, your story can be framed many ways.

A neighbor stands up at a community meeting and passionately claims, "This is about accountability!" He has named his frame. A congresswoman debates legislation saying, "This is not only about cutting costs, this is about justice." She too has named her frame. People debating the danger of a gas-drilling method argue whether it should be framed as an environmental, economic or a safety issue. Each of these frames says what the speaker hopes others will see as important or not important to the discussion.

Why does framing matter when telling your story as an advocate?

Because listeners may not frame your story as you intend. You may place your story within a frame of courage, injustice or community, but unless you name that frame, you risk audiences seeing it differently. When advocating with personal stories, you may need to specifically frame or "reframe" your story to help audiences hear it as you intend.

Being aware of how framing works helps you prepare for speaking and interview situations. Sometimes the context itself frames your story as you'd like; being included in the local news segment titled "Stories of Hope" may not require you to frame your story of hope. Other times you may need to frame or reframe your story so it is not misinterpreted, dismissed or distorted.

> *"This isn't just about me, this is a societal issue, this is a community issue. This is the story of thousands upon thousands of women. I'm talking about your sisters, your grandmothers, your aunts."*
> **Kathy Kastan, heart health advocate**

When and How to Reframe

Sometimes a reporter, intentionally or not, may frame your story negatively. The example on page 57 tells of an advocate who inadvertently lets reporters frame his story as one of grief and helplessness. See how that story is reframed as a one of courage and community on pages 59-60. Also see how Theresa Greenleaf frames her story on page 88.

There are a number of ways to construct framing statements:

- **Frame with the Theme.** "This is about how one person can help an entire community."
- **Frame Your Story as Story.** "This story is all-too familiar."
- **Frame Your Relationship to Audience.** "As a twenty-year member of this congregation…"
- **Frame Your Role and Identity.** "I'm speaking on behalf of the Green House Initiative."

Your Role and Identity within Regulatory Restrictions

Here's a case in which a particular frame may determine how you define your story. You may be asked to tell your story as part of an education or awareness-raising effort that has goals and key messages determined—or constrained—by jurisdiction, legal issues or government regulation. You'll likely need to stay within those constraints, and you may need to take extra care in the messages and their relationship to your story.

For example: you're sharing your story of an illness or health condition to an audience brought together by a company that makes a treatment for that condition. The Food and Drug Administration, the governmental body regulating the pharmaceutical industry, requires the company and its spokespersons—in this case, you—to provide "fair balance." In other words, if your story is about how beneficial a particular medicine was to you, you may also need to remind the audience that each person's case is unique, that there are various side effects and that it's important to consult with doctors. Other agencies, like the Federal Trade Commission, may also have requirements regarding transparency of sponsorship and disclosure of information in an interview. If there is a legal case pending, you may be asked to avoid giving specifics that might jeopardize the legal proceedings.

Your sponsoring organization will inform you of any parameters so you can share your story with impact, link it to messages and goals and frame it appropriately to remain within guidelines.

Use the following exercise, *Build and Name Your Frames*, to provide the right perspective on your story.

BUILD AND NAME YOUR FRAMES

Objective: *Practice statements that help audiences view your story appropriately.*

Use this exercise to:
- Find useful introductory statements
- Have ready-made responses to interview questions
- Be clear about what your story is and what it is not
- Be clear about how you want to be viewed in your story

There are a number of ways to build frames around stories or reframe them when necessary. Here are four options.

The exercise:
- Read the examples, then try your hand at your own framing statements.

Frame with the Theme. Name the value or belief underlying your story.

This is a story about my sister's courage. *This is about how important the community's support is.*	**Try it:**

Frame Your Story as a Story. When the words "This is a true story" appear on screen, we watch movies like *Norma Rae, Boys Don't Cry* or *The King's Speech* differently. It may help your audience to know something about your story *as* a story.

My story is an all-too familiar one... *When people hear my story they often say ...* *I decided last week it was time for me speak out...* *This is a story I love to tell...*	**Try it:**

BUILD AND NAME YOUR FRAMES (*continued*)

Frame with Your Role and/or Identity. How do you want your audiences to see you?

	Try it:
I'm a ten-year volunteer with Children in the Arts. *I am my father's primary caregiver and a spokesman for the National Alzheimer's Foundation.* *I'm a doctor, a dad, and a vocal advocate for children's rights.* *I'm someone who used to think I was invincible.*	

Frame with Your Relationship to the Audience. Draw a frame around all of you.

	Try it:
I am a member of this community and I've lived on this street for thirty-five years. *I am a member of this congregation.* *Like many of your television viewers, I care about the quality of our children's education.*	

Deliver Powerful Presentations

IN CHAPTER SEVEN

❏ Find the Most Useful Attitude to Be a Confident, Effective Speaker
❏ Prepare for the Audience, Context and Physical Environment
❏ Use a Basic Template for Your Talk or Speech
❏ Learn the Magic Recipe for Getting People to Act

From Talks to Keynotes

The term *public speaking* usually calls to mind the image of a person standing at a lectern before a seated audience, often with some projected visual aids on a screen behind. You may tell your story in this traditional speaking situation if you're a keynoter or guest speaker, but other settings—like the one in which Theresa Greenleaf told her story—may be very informal.

When Theresa's son Jack was in the third grade, there was a younger boy at his school with a severe allergy to peanuts. On two separate occasions he had such strong reactions that paramedics were called to the school. To guard against this happening again, the school nurse, Wendy, sent a note to the boy's homeroom parents asking them to refrain from packing peanut butter sandwiches or other nut products in lunches. Some of the parents didn't respond well to the request. At the time, Theresa says, there wasn't a great understanding of how serious allergic reactions or asthma attacks could be.

To increase awareness and persuade the parents to comply with the request, Nurse Wendy scheduled a meeting with the parents, invited an allergist to speak and asked a few parents of children with allergies to tell their stories. Theresa's son Jack had food allergies and asthma, so she had valuable experiences to share. She remembers:

Wendy was really smart about how she approached this. The meeting was in the school library, with a very intimate feel. It wasn't like she brought a parade of parents up to a podium to

*speak at the other parents. We just sat together; we were parents
among parents.*

*With my story I wanted to emphasize that it can be really scary—
and you learn that you need to rely on and trust other parents
and caregivers. I told what I had gone through trying to keep
Jack's environment allergen-free. I told some of the scary stories
and I told the absolute worst story: when I was taking him to the
doctor with an asthma episode and he lost consciousness in the
cab. I was already doing all kinds of stuff, I was leaving no stone
unturned and even then—this happened. I talked about the
ongoing effort and how appreciative I was of all the support
I got from the school and other parents. I framed it in the light
of appreciation.*

Whether you're sitting in a grade school library, standing at a lectern or canvassing door to door, it's all *public speaking*. And in every situation, your objective is the same: to be confident, comfortable and clear as you tell your story and deliver your messages.

Some people are born with a natural gift for public speaking; most of us require guidance and practice. But a little guidance and practice goes a long way in helping you feel more comfortable and confident in public speaking situations.

> *"I gave a talk at a local Baptist church. There were probably thirty women in the room; I didn't think it went that well. But after I finished, this woman came up to me and she said, 'In my life I have never heard a speech so powerful.' Months later she told me she had quit smoking. She'd been smoking for forty years. She quit smoking, and has not picked up a cigarette since. Well, I didn't even think that much of my presentation. But you can change people's lives without even knowing you're doing it."*
> **Kathy Kastan, heart health advocate**

Becoming an effective communicator is an ongoing process and the best advocates will tell you they never stop learning or looking for ways to

improve. Regardless of how you feel right now about speaking out—
whether "eager but anxious" or "committed and confident"—remember
these three Golden Rules:

1. Every opportunity to speak is an opportunity for growth.

2. Growth comes from setting goals—and forgiving the
   moments when you don't hit them.

3. Most public speaking anxieties are taken care of when
   you know what you want to say, why you're saying it and
   to whom.

Use the principles in this chapter and *Public Speaking: Tips and
Tools* (page 141) as you get ready to speak. Talk with other advocates
about what they've learned and the powerful experiences they've had
connecting with audiences. When you're ready, turn to the *Practice
Runs* in Chapter Nine to get ready for your next speaking opportunity.

Being Audience-Centered

Whether getting ready to speak to a roaring crowd or to a single person, the best advocates know that an important step in preparation is the one that takes them *outside* of themselves so they can consider the audience's perspective. Being audience-centered means finding out as much as you can about the audience—their attitudes, values, moods, knowledge—then tailoring what you say accordingly. It does *not* mean pandering to the audience or subordinating your own goals and passions. Being audience-centered simply means you've thought about how to best reach your audience so you communicate *with* them rather than talk *at* them.

When you know your audience, you know what story to tell. You know whether framing or reframing is necessary. And you stay focused on your key messages and goals. When you're audience-centered, you can *anticipate* both the challenges and opportunities of any speaking situation.

But there's an additional benefit to being audience-centered: the more you know about your audience and the more clearly you can visualize them as you prepare, the more confident and natural you'll be when you

Real Audiences Wear Clothes

You've probably heard the advice to practice speaking in front of a mirror or to imagine the audience in their underwear to calm your nerves. While a mirror's always helpful to check your appearance or see what a gesture looks like, don't get stuck there. When you get up in front of an audience you won't be speaking to your reflection, you'll be speaking to actual humans. And chances are they'll be clothed. Imagine your audience as they'll show up and you'll show up more comfortably.

speak. Most of the anxiety we feel about speaking comes from fear of the unknown: "What if they don't get it? What if they don't like it? What if they can't hear me?" Taking the time to address these questions and getting to know your audience *as you prepare* removes layer after layer of anxiety, helping you show up as your best self.

How much information you can gather about an audience depends upon the time you have to prepare and the access you have to them. You certainly can't know everything, and you'll have to make some assumptions. Still, gather as much information as you can to make those assumptions as accurate as possible—through observation, contact with others or online research. Here are some ways to gather this important information:

- **Ask.** If you're invited to speak, contact the organizers prior to the event. Ask if they would answer a few questions about the audience.

- **Reach out.** Contact other speakers who've addressed this audience.

- **Search online.** If the audience members belong to a group or organization, visit the group's website or read its published materials.

- **Watch**. Stand at the door and greet people as they arrive or position yourself so you can observe the audience and gauge their moods.

Use the *Prep Sheet* on page 153 as a guide to the kinds of information you can gather to create a full portrait of the audience.

This includes information like demographics (*Who are they? What ages, genders and cultural backgrounds are represented?*), situation (*Why are they here? How large is the audience? Is the setting formal or informal?*), attitudes (*How might they feel about you, your topic and your story? What do they expect to hear? What's their level of interest? What level of disclosure is appropriate?*) and values (*How do they think? What's important to them? What will seem familiar to them? What will seem foreign?*).

Being audience-centered helped Theresa Greenleaf anticipate how other parents might respond to her story. She planned accordingly:

I knew I had to be very careful of not painting a portrait of mothers of kids with allergies and asthma as being overprotective nut jobs. I also knew that I didn't want to "apologize," like when you make others aware that your child has the potential for anaphylactic shock and you get into that "Oh, gee. I'm sorry to have to tell you—I'm sorry that this is a potential pain in the neck."

What I really wanted to do was bring them into that cab with me, to share the moment of nearly losing my child.

The Speaking Context

Many factors can define a particular speaking context, from how you came to be here, to the function your story is asked to fulfill, to the time of day and what's going on in the news. All of these can affect how you tell your story and how it's received. Being aware of the speaking context means stepping back and surveying the "lay of the land." Factors that determine the speaking context include:

Timing. Some say it's everything. Where does your story fall during the day, on the agenda, in an awareness-raising campaign or in relation to what's going on in the news? All can affect how your audience hears and responds to you, and may require you to acknowledge the timing of your speech. For example, a hot news story that relates to yours may provide the perfect introduction. How your story relates to other stories on the agenda also may be worth noting.

Your Role. There are times when you're asked to "just tell" your story: perhaps an event where other speakers give organizational information or explain the advocacy goal. This was the case when Theresa Greenleaf spoke, joined by an allergist and the school nurse. Other times, you may be responsible not only for telling your story but also for speaking about the cause, organization or campaign. In Kathy Kastan's address at a fundraiser for the Cardiovascular Research Foundation (page 101), she served as a keynote speaker who was asked to share her story, to appear as an organizational spokesperson and to advocate for increased attention to women's health. Each situation requires something different from you in terms of what you say and how you say it, so consider "What is being asked of me in this particular situation?"

- *What is the event or occasion? What's the mood?*

- *What's my role? Am I the primary speaker? Am I responsible for saying anything in addition to my story? Who else will be speaking?*

- *What role is my story being asked to play in this event? When will I tell my story?*

Framing. Framing can include what happens right before and after you speak, how you are introduced, and even the banner hanging behind you. Any of these may provide the perfect frame to your story. You may also need to reframe. (See Chapter Six.)

Environment. Whether you're speaking in a hotel ballroom, on a wooden stage in the town square or in a grade school library, any physical environment presents both opportunities and challenges to telling your story effectively. The best way to know how you can make an environment work for you is to get an early look at it. Many of the challenges of a speaking environment can be eliminated with a little foresight and some minor adjustments, though others may require you to adapt "on the fly."

> "The fundraising event was the first time I told my story in a public speech. The only other times I'd spoken before were professionally, when I had been more removed from the audience, like on a stage, where I was not able to look at them eye to eye. Speaking at the fundraiser in the living room, everybody was right there. And anywhere I turned I could see every facial expression, not that far away from me. This was totally different."
> **Derek Cotton, advocate for cancer support services**

Here are some tips for managing the opportunities and challenges of the physical environment.

- **Be your audience.** Use your audience-centered perspective and imagine listening to and watching yourself speak.

- **Reduce distractions.** Look for potential barriers or interrupters: the mirrored wall behind the speaker's lectern, the noisy schoolyard next door, the large column in the middle of the room. Sit or stand where the audience will be: What gets your attention?

- **Set the stage.** A hotel ballroom with lighting, stage, microphone and lectern suggests a degree of formality you may want. But will your talk to a small group in the community center require the same arrangements? Possibly not. You may decide sitting in a circle is more conducive—as Nurse Wendy knew when she set the stage for the "parents among parents" in the school library.

- **If you don't like it, change it.** Consider how much control you have over the physical environment and aspects of the context, such as timing or framing. You may find you have more control than you thought. Be proactive in making the speaking situation work best for you, your story and your audience. Move the lectern, use that poster as a backdrop, suggest speaking before or after the break or find out how you will be introduced.

Use the *Prep Sheets* starting on page 156 to assess the speaking context and aspects of the physical environment.

Strategic Structures

Whether you're "just telling" your story or telling your story *and* conveying other substantial information, your speech should follow the same basic structure: Intro, Body and Conclusion. Each of these three structural parts has specific ingredients. And they're just that: ingredients—not a recipe. How you meet the essential criteria of an Intro, Body or Conclusion is one of the most creative aspects of public speaking.

The Introduction

Compared to the rest of your presentation, the introduction is short. It may only be a couple sentences. At minimum, an introduction should:

- **Gain and focus your audience's attention.** This may be a simple pause before you begin, a moment of interaction with your audience or a scene from your story. Try using a headline or a hook. Be creative, but make sure your attention-getter is appropriate to your cause, occasion and your individual speaking style.

- **Establish your purpose for speaking.** This may be a framing statement ("I'm here as a representative of…"), a clear statement of your goal ("I'm happy to share what this program has meant to me and my family") or what you intend for your audience ("This is information important to your health and well being").

- **Preview your structure or key points.** If you're taking the audience on a journey, the preview is where you spread the map out on the table, point out the stops along the way and describe the final destination.

The Body

The body of your presentation either includes:

- Your story, or

- Your story and additional content structured around key messages

Just as there are many ways to tell your story, there are many ways to structure the body of your speech. Here are three options for weaving your story, key messages and supporting material together.

Body Option #1: Story as Backbone

Use your story as the foundation of the body, bringing in key messages or supporting material as appropriate.

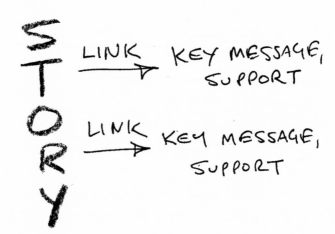

Body Option #2: Story as Proof Point

Use your story to illustrate the key messages and other content.

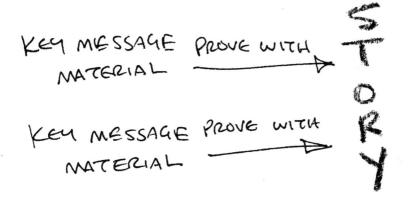

Body Option #3: Story as Envelope

Begin and end with your story, using it as the wrapping that contains your key messages and other content.

The Conclusion

Like the introduction, the conclusion is brief. At minimum, it should:

- **Remind the audience of the key messages.** Make the most of this, your last chance. Audiences remember final words; make them memorable. Relate your conclusion back to your introduction as a way of "tying up the package."

- **Present any "calls to action."** Tell your audience specifically what you want them to do after listening to you.

Use this basic structure as a template for organizing any advocacy presentation: long or short, formal or informal, talk or keynote. At right is how heart health advocate Kathy Kastan's address at a fundraiser for the Cardiovascular Research Foundation followed the structure.

Introduction	
• Grab and focus audience attention	Kathy began with a hook and the theme of her speech: *At forty-one, I never thought about my own mortality. My attention was elsewhere.* *When I started having shortness of breath, fatigue, pain in my upper left back and occasional pain down my left arm, I noticed that something was changing in my body. But even having those symptoms off and on for eight months didn't get me to pay attention. Nor did I tell anyone.*
• Establish your purpose • Preview your story or key messages	*How many of you truly pay attention to your bodies, your emotions and your health?*
Body	
• Tell your crafted, focused story	Kathy used her story as the "envelope," taking her audience through her journey of unrecognized symptoms of heart disease, misdiagnosis, correct diagnosis, bypass surgery and return to health. Throughout, she echoed her main theme: *And then one day while I was on vacation in the majestic Colorado Rockies I collapsed on a sidewalk with not vague symptoms but classic Hollywood heart attack symptoms (front-to-back chest pain, etc.). Well, that got my attention. It got my husband's attention too. I went to a second cardiologist who confirmed that I had been misdiagnosed but unfortunately he really wasn't paying attention either and sent me on my way. It wasn't until I collapsed a second time that I got his attention.* After delivering supporting material about heart disease in women and her sponsoring organization, she returned to her story to stress the importance of "paying attention."
Conclusion	
• Remind the audience of your key messages • Present any "call to action"	Kathy gave her audience a number of ways to "pay attention," including knowing the risks of heart disease and visiting the website of the organization she represented.

Use the *Prep Sheet* on page 159 to plan the structure of your next speech.

A Recipe for Action

W hile the basic template using Intro, Body and Conclusion gives you a list of ingredients, Monroe's Motivated Sequence is an actual recipe—a tried-and-true formula for moving an audience to act. Dr. Allen Monroe of the University of Chicago popularized this five-step model in the 1940s. Next time you watch television or online media, notice how many commercials still follow this structure: Attention, Need, Satisfaction, Visualization and Action.

- **Attention.** As in any good introduction, start by gaining the audience's attention by relating the topic directly to them.

- **Need.** Make the audience feel the need for a positive change. Focus on how your information or story demonstrates a serious problem. In addition to your story, use strong supporting materials—statistics, visuals, quotes from others. By the time you finish this step, listeners should be deeply concerned and ready to hear your solutions.

- **Satisfaction.** Provide a solution to the problem, map out the positive change for which you advocate. Depending upon the context, you may present detailed information, showing how the solution will work.

- **Visualization.** An important step: have your audience visualize the benefits of your plan. This is where you use vivid imagery to illustrate that better world for which you advocate, helping them see how much better it will be once that positive change has been achieved.

- **Action.** Say exactly what you want the audience to do and how they should go about doing it. Remind them once more of the seriousness of the problem and the need for change.

Many advocates find Monroe's Motivated Sequence useful when structuring specific persuasive appeals, as when asking for contributions or inspiring others to join their cause. A good example of this structure is Scott Harrison's speech at the Big Omaha tech conference. At this meeting of movers and shakers on the "Silicon Prairie," Scott told the story of how he founded **charity: water** with the goal of bringing clean drinking water to billions. The conference audience of five hundred was already supportive and sympathetic, having contributed $5,000 for the organization prior to the conference. Following Scott's speech, another $10,000 was raised. Using personal experience and moving photographs to tell the story of his organization, Scott motivated the audience to do more. You can find a link to Scott's forty-five-minute presentation at www.livingproofadvocacy.com. Here's how he fulfilled Monroe's five steps:

Attention Gain the audience's attention. Relate the topic directly to the audience.	Everyone knew Scott was there to talk about water and his organization. He thanks them for the $5,000 they've raised, telling how it would be used. Then he surprises them: *I'm going to start by first telling you about my mother.* He tells of his childhood, caring for his mother who had a compromised immune system, and of his rebellion at age eighteen: *I spent my life looking after her, now it was time to look out for Number One. Grew my hair long, joined a band, moved to New York City. I wanted to be rich and famous and I wanted to do all the things I was told I wasn't able to do. And I got really good at that.* We follow him from his "selfish and arrogant" life as a nightclub promoter, to his feelings of spiritual bankruptcy, to his volunteering for a humanitarian organization offering free medical care in Africa, where: *I got my first taste of dirty water in Liberia.*
Need Make the audience feel the need for a positive change.	He tells why he decided to focus his new charitable self on water issues: *... one of the most important issues facing the poor today. It was connected to so many other things I'd seen. It was a root cause. It was the reason kids weren't able to get an education.* Graphically, both visually and verbally, Scott relates story after story of what he saw in West Africa. Statistics, video of parasites in drinking water, stories of families carrying forty-pound Jerry cans of contaminated water and teenage girls whose lives are defined by deficiency: *...kids grow up and their spines are bent 'cause they started carrying water at the age of five.*
Satisfaction Provide a solution to the problem, map out the positive change for which you advocate.	With the audience primed for a solution: *The good news is that there are solutions and we know how to help a billion people.* He shows the kinds of solutions **charity: water** has funded: wells, filters, rainwater catchment. He tells how the wells are built, tells stories of the local community rallying around the projects. He reminds the audience that the $5,000 they raised paid for the drilling of wells, each one providing water for more than 250 people.

Visualization
Have your audience visualize the benefits of your plan.
	With his key message that "water is everything," Scott vividly shows what happens when a community gets clean water:
	    It's awesome when you hit water. It's one of the greatest things…water really changes everything. We believe this to our core. Clean water brings hope into communities, it brings life. It restores dignity to women, to kids, to teenage girls. It puts so much time back into the community. Disease rates start plummeting when clean water is brought into a community. And we can prove it. And we can show it can be done.
	Scott then tells how **charity: water** came to be, their fundraising strategies, their successes, their mistakes and—most importantly—he tells stories of how individuals have creatively raised money: from kids "giving up their birthdays" to four guys walking across the U.S. to:
	    Jodie Landers, a mom from Muscatine, Iowa. She adopted two kids from Sierra Leone, went to her church, went to schools, said, "Kids around the world need clean water." Raised $300,000 in her small town.

Action
Say exactly what you want the audience to do and how they should go about doing it.
	Briefly and succinctly:
	    So I'd like to ask you guys: will you make this your story? What can you do to help? Some of you can get your companies involved. Everyone in this room could give up a birthday.
	Visibly moved, he concludes:
	    If not us, who? And if not now, when?

Use the *Prep Sheet* on pages 160-161 to map out your action plan, according to Monroe's recipe.

Ready to practice? Use the *Practice Runs* in Chapter Nine to get ready for your next talk.

Give Great
Interviews

IN CHAPTER EIGHT

❏ Take All the Opportunities Offered by a Media Interview
❏ Get to Know Your Target Audience
❏ Prepare for the Interview Context
❏ Amaze Your Friends and Family with Your Media Skills

The Media Opportunity

As an advocate, you have the *one* thing every reporter, blogger and journalist wants. You have a story. You have a story that's been crafted to be engaging and memorable, a story told genuinely with the audience in mind. This is precisely what media interviewers look for because what they fear most is that they'll speak with someone who is unprepared and unresponsive. That's not you.

You just need to make sure the story you tell is the one the reporter reports.

From start to finish—from taking a media call to the wrap-up question and last few seconds of a broadcast—interviews are about opportunity. Advocates sometimes dodge media interviews because they assume the reporter will be a barrier to delivering their messages or story. While it's true some interviews can be challenging, in most instances you and the reporter are focused on the very same goal: a compelling story. An interview is a wide expanse of opportunity, not a minefield. To give a great interview, you need to be prepared and alert, ready to seize every moment of what will likely be a very short time.

Before becoming an advocate for stricter laws against distracted driving, Loren Vaillancourt was uncomfortable with any type of public speaking. The death of her brother in an auto accident changed that:

> *Right after Kelson was killed, it was so strange, because I had this*
> *overwhelming feeling that I had to tell his story, and I had to do*
> *it for him, and that I could possibly save lives. It wasn't the easiest*

*thing to accept right away, to be honest with you, because—good
gracious—I never in a million years could see myself doing as
much speaking as I am.*

It wasn't long, however, before Loren found herself speaking
frequently to local and national media, including CBS' *The Early Show*.
As the reigning Miss South Dakota, Loren gave reporters a compelling
angle: a pageant queen with an intimate perspective on an issue getting
national attention. With her key message that "these accidents are
100% preventable," Loren gave audiences a very effective advocacy
story: focused, crafted, framed, practiced and pointing to positive
change. Her 3½-minute appearance on *The Early Show* is a great
example of the opportunity in a media interview. View the segment
at www.livingproofadvocacy.com.

As with any type of successful communication, giving a great
interview is a matter of anticipation and preparation. First, you want to
know your audience so you can keep them firmly in mind. Next, assess
the interview context by knowing the type of interview, the setting and
the interviewer. Then, applying some basic media skills, give the
reporter a story that will not only reach and move audiences, but also
advance your advocacy mission.

Use the principles in this chapter and *Media Interviews: Tips and
Tools* (page 163) as you get ready for your interview. Watch other
advocates like Loren online and on television to see how the best make
it look natural. When you're ready, use the *Practice Runs* in Chapter
Nine to get ready for your next media opportunity.

Know Your Target Audience

W hen you give a speech you have direct access to your audience, the people who watch, listen and respond to you.

In media interviews, you rarely have direct access to your audience. The interviewer *serves as the filter* through which your messages pass to reach the viewers, listeners or readers.

Your target audience—made up of media consumers—is where you want to focus: on the people who listen to the newscast, pick up the magazine or watch the talk show. Knowing your target audience is vital to deciding how you tell your story and what key messages you stress. Build a mental image of your target audience by gathering as much information as you can about why they'll be interested in what you have to say. Here are some ideas of how to gather information about your target audience.

- **Preview.** If you're being interviewed for TV, radio or the Internet, preview the show or blog to see how the media outlet speaks to the target audience and what they report on. Look online for archived videos or audio interviews, especially those related to your topic.

- **Read.** For a print piece, read the articles by the reporter who is interviewing you and review past issues of the magazine or newspaper (often available online).

- **Surf.** Visit the media outlet's website. Look under "Advertise With Us" and you may find a summary of the target audience (median age, gender, education and interests).

- **Test.** Do you know people who read, watch, or listen to the media you'll be addressing? Try out your story and key messages on them. Ask what they like best about the media.

Use the *Prep Sheet* on page 176 as a guide to the kind of information you can gather to paint a picture of your target audience: demographics (*Who are they? How do they engage with this media outlet?*), interests (*Why are they interested in this media, this topic?*) and attitudes (*How might they feel about you, your topic or your story?*).

The Interview Context

The most common interview situation is one that will support your message of positive change. These human interest articles or public service segments may promote an upcoming event, feature a hometown angle or be part of a large awareness or education campaign. The tone of these interviews is supportive and allows you to tell your story well and deliver key messages clearly. When Loren Vaillancourt appeared on *The Early Show*, the news anchor cast Loren's story as important living proof of the need for stricter laws, opening with "There's a troubling new report out this morning about distracted driving," and closing with "All it takes is a split second for you to remove your eyes from the road." All Loren needed to provide was the compelling evidence.

But many factors can affect how the dynamics of an interview play out, so as you prepare it's important to step back and consider the wider context. Think of it as finding out what direction the river is flowing, and at what speed, before you push off from shore.

- *What is the reason for the interview?*

- *What is the focus of the interview?*

- *What information am I responsible for conveying? Are there organizational messages I must deliver?*

- *How do I want my story to be framed?*

Factors that determine the interview context include:

Timing. In Loren's case, the timing was perfect. Her interview aired the same day the Department of Transportation launched a major awareness campaign on the dangers of distracted driving. But depending upon the nature of your cause and what else is happening in the world of news, it's possible the interview atmosphere may be less than supportive. Your topic or the organization you represent may be considered controversial by the media, and the reporter may look to challenge you. Popular attitudes toward your topic may influence the reporter's stance and the questions asked.

Your Role. If, for example, you appear as an official spokesperson, that carries certain responsibilities for delivering organizational messages and, perhaps, restrictions on what you can and cannot say. See *Your Role and Identity within Regulatory Restrictions*, page 84.

The Reporter. Reporters come in all shapes and sizes, personality types and skill levels. They may know quite a bit about your topic or be unprepared. One thing they have in common is this: They're under pressure to capture a good story, on deadline. To help them get what they want, on time, see *Handling Questions from a Reporter*, page 174.

Framing. How the media frames your story may or may not match how you want it to be framed. Your story may be framed as confident advocacy or hesitant disclosure. You may be framed as fierce crusader or tragic victim. Loren Vaillancourt *could* have been framed many ways in her media appearance: grieving sister, Miss America contestant, angered survivor. Instead, the news anchor framed Loren as a dedicated advocate: "You're out there speaking to people about this all the time. Do you feel like being out there, speaking out about it…is that making an impact?"

Form of Media. Print, television, web or radio—each requires certain skills and special attention to how you present yourself and your story. Each also changes the dynamic between you and the reporter, and you and your target audience.

Use *Media Interviews: Tips and Tools* (page 163) to assess and manage the interview context, and to prepare for radio, television, web and print interviews.

Stay In Story and On Message

You know your story, your key messages and who your target audience is. Now it's time to practice some fundamental interview techniques to ensure that, no matter how an interview goes, no matter what questions a reporter asks, you'll be able to tell your story powerfully and make your points clearly.

A media interview—whether for print or broadcast—is not a simple question-and-answer exchange between you and a reporter. It's not a conversation—although it should sound like one—or an interrogation. It's an opportunity for you to deliver specific messages to specific audiences through the filter of a reporter. Think of the interview process as talking *through* the reporter to your audience.

> "A skill I've learned throughout the year of media appearances is to come up with a 5-minute version. And then a 1-minute version. And then a 30-second version. And then a 10-second version. So no matter what kind of environment you're put in, you're always able to get the most important points across."
> **Loren Vaillancourt, advocate for stricter distracted driving laws**

Since you were probably contacted by or asked to speak to the media because you have a story to tell, reporters will often ask questions that let you get quickly to your story. But you can't always count on the right questions being asked. Even if you have a good idea of the kinds of questions a reporter may ask, you won't know exactly *how* they'll be asked. So don't head into an interview hoping and waiting for the *right* questions. If you passively engage with an interviewer, simply responding to the questions, you risk giving him or her complete control over the interview's direction. In extreme cases, when a reporter has a particular agenda that is counter to yours, being a passive interviewee allows the reporter to tell her or his story, not yours. (See the example on page 57.)

QUESTION → RESPONSE → QUESTION → RESPONSE

INTERVIEWER IN CONTROL

Instead, actively participate in the interview, viewing each question as an opportunity to tell your story and deliver your messages.

QUESTION → RESPONSE   QUESTION → RESPONSE   QUESTION
↓ KEY ↗   ↓ KEY ↗
MESSAGE   MESSAGE

YOU IN CONTROL

By using some simple interview techniques, you can control the interview and make sure the target audience hears your story and key messages as you intend. Guiding and shaping the interview to best serve your advocacy goals requires you to practice Deflecting/Blocking, Bridging, Flagging and Headlining.

Deflecting/Blocking and Bridging

Sometimes a reporter's question can steer the interview to places you'd rather not go: to topics that don't relate to your story, uncomfortable areas or information you'd rather not include as part of the interview. Certain statements by the reporter too (such as an incorrect paraphrase of something you've said), might lead to misinformation, off-topic

117

discussions or an inappropriate frame to your story. To avoid this, you may need to *deflect* or *block* a question or statement, then *bridge* to a more desirable territory.

Bridging means moving smoothly from where the interview is to where you'd like it to go. Before you bridge, however, you may need to redirect a question or statement by deflecting it. Other times you may need to completely block a statement before you bridge back to your story or message. The objective is to respond and bridge quickly so you don't give too much attention or weight to the question or statement you're deflecting or blocking. For example:

Deflect and Bridge

That's a question a lot of people have, but what's really behind that question is...

That's really the rare case. What we see much more often is...

Rather than that, it's really a matter of access. Let me tell you the good news...

Block and Bridge

That's not my area of expertise, but what I can tell you is...

I can't go into those kinds of details, but what I can tell about my experience...

I don't see it that way. The way I see it is...

Notice how, in these examples, the response does not repeat the incorrect or negative language the reporter may have used. Use nondescript pronouns or adjectives like *that* or *those kinds* rather than give currency to the reporter's phrasing.

Even when the interview is going well, you may need to bridge to your story or messages to ensure they're part of the interview. Again, don't wait for the right question to be asked. Bridge with simple statements such as:

That's a great point. Another is…
Let me just add…
Let me put that into perspective…
What I'm really here to talk about is…
I think your audience would also be interested to know…
That's another great example of how…

Interviewer: *In terms of heart disease, your arteries are either clogged or they're not clogged, right? Is that right?*

Kathy: *Well, no. There are different types of problems that can happen with your heart and there are different types of heart disease you can have…*

Kathy Kastan, heart health advocate, blocking and bridging during a radio interview

Flagging

Flagging is the verbal equivalent of using a highlighter to draw attention to the words and statements that will make reporters and audiences sit up and listen. When you "raise a flag," you'll hear the clacking of a computer keyboard on the other end of the call as the reporter makes notes. Your radio listeners will keep the car radio on after parking. Your television audiences will pause in their walks across the living room and stop in front of the screen to hear what you're saying. By flagging, you let your audiences and the reporter know the most important points about the story and your messages. Some flagging words and phrases are:

What's most important for people to understand…
Here's why people need to hear this story…
What we really want to make clear is…
Here's what I think your listeners will be most interested in knowing…
This is the most dangerous misconception people have…

119

Headlining

Media interviews, whether print or broadcast, begin with the most important information at the top, followed by information that supports or explains. So provide the interviewer with a headline early in your interview, if not immediately. Headlining is absolutely critical in a broadcast interview. These are typically very brief and you want to ensure they highlight your key messages. Even in a print interview, headlining helps the reporter understand what the main theme of your story is; this process may even provide the actual headline for the written piece.

Want a Great Headline?

Turn to Chapter Five, *Craft Your Story*, for tips on creating memorable hooks.

The next exercise, *Bridge from Anywhere*, was introduced to us by one of the advocates in our workshop.

If you're ready to practice for your upcoming interview, turn to the *Practice Runs* in Chapter Nine.

EXERCISE

BRIDGE FROM ANYWHERE

Objective: Practice getting from anywhere to your key messages and your story.

Use this exercise to:
- Find natural links to your key messages
- Make bridges "second nature," not forced
- Amaze or amuse your family and friends

We once reconnected with an advocate who had been through our workshop a year or so prior. She was a WomenHeart Champion, a woman with heart disease who was out speaking in her community and to the media, telling her story and delivering key educational messages about women and heart disease: Early detection. Accurate diagnosis. Proper treatment. She told us, "Thanks to you, I'm driving my family crazy."

"How so?" we asked.

She then told us how she practiced bridging at home. "I take whatever my family says to me and try to bridge back to my story or to the WomenHeart messages. For example, my husband's heading out to a meeting and he asks me whether there's gas in the car. I tell him that I noticed on the way home that the tank was low, so I stopped and filled it up. Then I bridge: 'which is yet another example of the importance of early detection, accurate diagnosis and proper treatment.'"

We thought her exercise was brilliant, so we've been advising others to give it a shot ever since.

The exercise:
- Deftly bridge from something your friends say to your advocacy story and mission.

121

Chapter Nine

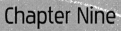

Practice

IN CHAPTER NINE

❏ Find Out How Speaking as an Advocate is Like Jazz
❏ Learn Healthy Practice Habits

Speak Improvisationally

On the continuum of speaking styles, *impromptu* lives on one end (speaking off-the-cuff with little or no preparation) with *manuscript speaking* at the other (speaking from a script or teleprompter). Each style is appropriate at certain times. But when telling a personal story, these two modes are rarely desirable. You can't be totally impromptu or you'll risk presenting a raw, unprepared story; if you script it, you could come across as canned.

Somewhere between these two extremes is the style of speaking that enables you to be practiced, flexible and natural. It's a style that requires you to decide key messages, how you'll tell your story, even specific wording you might use—but what you say may come out differently each time you speak—like natural conversation. It's a style that's adaptable to most situations, from informal talks to formal addresses to telephone interviews to on-camera appearances. Usually called *extemporaneous* speaking, it's more accurate to name it *improvisational*.

Not improvisational as in "creating something out of nothing" or "without preparation."

> **Advocacy Stories Are Practiced**
>
> Jazz saxophonist Charlie Parker said it best: "You've got to learn your instrument. Then, you practice, practice, practice. And then, when you finally get up there on the bandstand, forget all that and just wail." This same philosophy applies to your preparation for advocacy. Speaking in public, whether you're interacting with an audience or a reporter, is a full-body experience involving your story, your voice, your body, your mindset. The sooner you begin to practice that instrument, the more confident and clear you will be in the actual moment—when you "just wail."

Improvisational like jazz.

A jazz musician playing *My Funny Valentine* knows the melody will always remain the same, with notes that need to be hit each time it's played. But the musician improvises around the melody, playing it a bit differently each time, keeping the basic song structure yet bringing to it his or her unique voice, artistry, expression and personality.

When you speak, you improvise around your story and key messages. What you say may change slightly or even dramatically each time, *but the tune remains the same.* Improvisational speaking, with its blend of preparation and spontaneity, enables you to speak naturally and focus attention where it should be: on your audience, on your story, on your messages and goals.

Depending upon your comfort level and experience, improvisational speaking may sound intimidating. Don't worry. Everything you do to prepare to tell your story as an advocate—choosing what to tell, focusing your story on your goals and messages, knowing who your audience is and practicing—also prepares you to be more improvisational.

Part of the unease some feel in embracing improvisational speaking comes from a strong desire for perfection,

> *"I've never memorized anything word for word because, good grief, if you started getting off track, the rest of whatever you're trying to say is lost. So the most effective way that I've found is just to make bullet points and an outline. These are the points I want to talk about. And then just go from your heart—because people are going to take so much better to you and your message if they can tell that you're speaking from your heart and not from memorized words."*
> **Loren Vaillancourt, advocate for stricter distracted driving laws**

> *"Don't script it. Tell your whole story to yourself, the entire thing, then find the parts that you really feel are important. Look at how much time you have and prioritize those points: these are the ones you hit, these are the ones you don't. Stick to that—and just tell it from your heart. Say, 'This is what this means to me.' Then everything else will follow. Say it with feeling. And don't fake it."*
> **Derek Cotton, advocate for cancer support services**

a feeling that if a word doesn't come out quite right or a phrase is forgotten, you've blown the whole speech or interview. Rarely is this the case. An audience is not aware of the perfection in your head. They only know the communication that's happening between you and them. Aim for connection, not perfection. As jazz saxophonist Coleman Hawkins said about making music, "if you don't make mistakes, you're not really trying." Accept that there may be imperfections; correct them when necessary and move on. It's worth it to get to the more natural and conversational style that is improvisational speaking.

Good Practice Habits

Ultimately, you'll find the practice methods that work best for you. But here are some guiding principles to keep in mind as you find your own routine.

Define Your Individual Style

Ask a roomful of people to describe how they'd like to be viewed as advocates, and chances are you'll hear a lot of similar responses: clear, confident, effective, engaging. But keep asking and you'll start to hear how differently people describe their individual styles: one person wants to be perceived as warm, another as forceful. One hopes to comes across as precise, another as energizing. As you prepare and practice your advocacy skills, think about how you want people to describe *you* as an advocate. What is *your* individual style and voice? Use these tips to find out.

- **Ask.** Get into the habit of asking your peers and partners for honest assessments of your effectiveness and whether you're coming across as you'd like.

- **Challenge.** Be as clear about how you *don't* want to be perceived as you are about how you *do* want to be perceived.

- **Write it.** Keep a written description with you of what you want your individual style to be. Refer to it as you practice.

- **Gut-check.** Most of us know when something feels artificial. Listen to your gut. If the words or expressions you're using feel forced, ask whether you're speaking naturally or imitating someone else's style.

- **Assess.** Use your written description as the gauge by which you measure your progress. When you watch or listen to your recorded practice or appearance, ask: What am I doing that creates the style I want? What am I doing that detracts from it?

Internalize Your Structure

The more you tell your story as an advocate, the more likely you are to set some phrases, sentences and even paragraphs to memory. After all, you've crafted certain language specifically to engage your audiences, and you've composed a few excellent headlines to hook them. But it's doubtful you'll ever memorize an entire story, speech or interview appearance word for word. Speaking improvisationally, though, you have in mind a basic structure, a roadmap, that remains fixed regardless of the particular speech or interview you're giving. Just as a jazz musician sets the notes of the song and chords to memory to guide improvisation, aim to *internalize the basic structure* of your story, speech or interview. That structure might be the arrangement of the pieces of your experience, an outline of your talk's intro, body and conclusion, or the key messages that guide your interview responses. Use these pointers to work on internalizing your structure:

- **Map it.** Use your *Story Map* or sketch a skeletal outline to set the structure in your visual memory.

- **Practice aloud.** Vocalizing and moving or gesturing as you practice helps "set it in the body."

- **Visualize.** Do a mental run-through of your talk or interview as you sit calmly or as you fall asleep.

- **U.A.M.D.** That means "Use A Mnemonic Device." Come up with a clever memory aid like spelling a short word with the initial letters of your key messages.

- **Talk structure.** Use the *Practice Run* on page 133 and try speaking *just* your structure: "I'll start off using the sentence about my trip to Italy. I'll preview my talk with… then I'll hit my first key message…then I'll transition to my second key message…"

Harness the Butterflies

We've all felt nervousness and know how disconcerting it can be. However, your goal is not to eliminate nervous energy. You want to *channel* this surge of adrenaline in a productive way. Think of it as a personal reservoir of extra energy you need to bring passion to your advocacy and to stay focused. Your goal is to learn to tap that reservoir.

"Harnessing the butterflies" is not something that happens with a flick of a switch. It comes with practice and experience, and all the preparation outlined in *Living Proof* is aimed at increasing your confidence and comfort. Here are some additional reminders:

- **Practice aloud.** Have we stressed this enough? It's the only way to get your body, voice and mind ready. For speeches, it's how you clock your time; for interviews, it's how you practice responses to potential questions.

- **Be realistic.** You don't have to be perfect. Remember that audiences and interviewers are generally supportive and forgiving.

- **Use relaxation techniques.** Breathe deeply. Shake out your hands and arms. Roll your shoulders. Roll your head. Reduce the tension in your throat by yawning and humming.

- **Be healthy.** Get lots of rest and drink plenty of water the day you are to speak. Speaking publicly is a physically engaging activity. Train for it.

- **Use video recordings whenever possible.** Okay, it may be a little painful at first to watch yourself practice speaking or being interviewed, but video recording is an invaluable addition to your preparation. It's most useful for becoming aware of things you *don't* think about when speaking: word choice, repetitive phrases, distracting gestures or stances, eye contact, an ill-fitting ensemble. If you really want to see whether you pace too much or have an unconscious nervous gesture, play the video in fast motion and watch how motions repeat. The only way to know how you look on camera is to be on camera.

EIGHT PRACTICE RUNS

Objective: Approach your practice from a variety of directions.

Use this exercise to:
- Get ready for specific talks or interviews
- Become more improvisational
- Generate content and language
- Guard against a canned and over-rehearsed style

Throughout *Living Proof*, we call your preparation for advocacy *practice* rather than *rehearsal*. Rehearsal typically implies a trial performance that approximates the situation as fully as possible: you're in the environment, wearing what you'll wear, using your full voice and energy and running it from start to finish, perhaps before an audience. While it's certainly possible you may need that kind of rehearsal for an event or appearance, the majority of speaking or interview situations you prepare for probably require a more improvisational style. For that reason, we recommend taking a *practice run* approach to your preparation.

The following *Practice Runs* ask you to approach your preparation in a variety of ways. The more ways you practice your story, the more improvisational and confident you will be. For all of these *Practice Runs*, record and make notes of your insights or work with a partner.

The exercise:

Practice Run #1: The Better World
- Imagine sitting or standing comfortably with an interviewer. She or he is intensely interested in your mission and story. Set a timer at three minutes, and imagine he or she asks you these questions:

What is the change you want to see in the world? What is that better world like?

- Keep talking for the full three minutes and describe as fully as you can what the change is you imagine and what that better world looks like. Use these phrases to begin and return to them if you get stuck:

EIGHT PRACTICE RUNS (*continued*)

I am advocating for...
I am advocating in order to...
What I want to see happen is...
By telling my story I hope...

Practice Run #2: What You Need to Know

- Imagine your audience is in the room with you. Sit or stand comfortably, set a timer for three minutes, and start speaking. The theme of this free-telling is: "Why it's important for you to hear my experience."

- Keep talking for the full three minutes. Use one of these phrases to begin and return to them if you get stuck:

It's important for you to hear my experience because...
Here's how my experience relates to you...
I think you may be surprised to know this about my experience...

Practice Run #3: Speak the Start

- If preparing for a speech, practice just the first thirty seconds. Practice sitting or standing as you will at the start. Think about what happens right before you speak. Concentrate on starting strong.

- If preparing for an interview, practice your very first answer. Imagine the interviewer asks you an open-ended question: "What happened?"

Practice Run #4: Speak the Finish

- If preparing for a speech, practice just the last thirty seconds. Practice sitting or standing as you will at the end of your talk. Think about what happens right afterward. Concentrate on ending strong.

- If preparing for an interview, practice your last answer. Imagine the interviewer says, "We only have thirty seconds left. Is there anything else you want our audience to know?"

EIGHT PRACTICE RUNS (*continued*)

Practice Run #5: Talk the Structure

- Focus on the structure of your story or speech, or the key messages you will stress in your interview. Practice speaking the structure, for example:

I begin with the startling statistic, then explain why I'm here today. I preview my key messages, then transition to my story...

The three key messages I'm going to return to in the interview are...

Practice Run #6: Tarzan-ing

- Think about how you've chosen to tell your story and the order in which you'll tell events or episodes. Focus on the *transitions* between moments or events. Practice just the transitions (like Tarzan, swinging from vine to vine).

- If preparing for a talk or speech, think of the structure. Focus on the transitions between Intro, Body and Conclusion and practice just those transitions.

- If preparing for an interview, use the *Bridge from Anywhere* exercise on page 121.

- This is a particularly useful *Practice Run* if you're working with visual aids. Practice just the transitions from visual to visual.

Practice Run #7: Soft Ball

- If preparing for an interview, write a list of questions you *hope* the reporter will ask you. Make them open-ended questions ("What happened?") or directly related to your advocacy goal ("Why is this important?" "What do you want people to do?").

- Have a partner ask you the questions and practice responding. Practice multiple responses.

EIGHT PRACTICE RUNS (*continued*)

Practice Run #8: Hard Ball
- If preparing for an interview, write a list of questions you hope the reporter *does not* ask you. Look at *Handling Questions from a Reporter* (page 174) for types of challenging questions. Think of questions that would take the interview in the wrong direction or directly challenge your advocacy.

- Have a partner ask you the questions and practice responding. Practice multiple responses.

Chapter Ten

Where Stories Lead

Stepping Forward, Making a Difference

The reasons advocates go public with personal experiences are as varied as the stories they tell. So too are the places advocacy takes them.

Like heart health advocate Kathy Kastan, your original motivation may have come from a sense of giving back. She began as a spokeswoman for the organization that helped her find proper treatment for heart disease. Now she has a new career as an advocate and educator. Like Theresa Greenleaf, mom of a child with allergies, sharing your story may be a one-time act required by specific circumstances like a grade school parent's meeting. Someone may have seen the value in your story even before you did, as when cancer survivor Derek Cotton was asked to help advocate for a cancer support organization. You may be in a leadership position like Scott Harrison or Ocean Robbins, using your story as an example of your organization's mission, as Scott and Ocean do when they advocate for clean drinking water or for environmental stewardship. Like Loren Vaillancourt, you may speak to national media or small groups in high school gymnasiums, as she often does when she advocates for stricter distracted driving laws. Or, like Becky Blanton, you may find yourself on the world stage.

Becky had the rare opportunity to first tell her story of homelessness in Oxford, England, at the TED Global Conference:

It felt scary. It felt exciting. It felt lonely. It felt sad. It felt liberating. I cycled through each of those emotions over and over. I remember thinking, "If I do this, there's no going back."

You can view a video of her speech at TED.com (www.ted.com)—which means Becky's story now reaches an enormous audience. She's heard from scores of others who have found themselves in similar circumstances, and her hopeful message that "we are not defined by where we live" has touched many.

Her speech has also rubbed people the wrong way. Entering the complex conversation about homelessness via the platform afforded her by TED.com, Becky has also heard criticism about everything from the details of her story to not properly framing the issue to the presentation itself.

Becky's experience is an important reminder that there is always a degree of risk when you step forward—and how important it is to stay focused. Becky advises:

Anyone who tells their story has to realize that people may criticize. You have to come to terms with that and be strong in who you are. Having a support system in place is really helpful. Focus on the positive. Revisit your motives.

It's just as important to maintain your focus when you are successfully reaching audiences, when you deliver a lot of powerful presentations and give countless great interviews. As the value of your story is recognized, you may be called upon to speak more frequently, and may enjoy a measure of local or national recognition. Still, it's important to maintain your vision of what drove you to speak out—the people on whose behalf you advocate. Keep them at the core of your advocacy, and the focus will stay where it should be: on the positive change —the difference you want to make.

Our final bit of advice comes from a sentiment we hear expressed by many advocates who've been out speaking and giving interviews: be prepared to be surprised. No matter how much anyone prepares you for telling your story, you can't know how it will go until it happens. For Kathy Kastan, that surprise came the first time she spoke out:

The first time I told my story in public was at the Jewish Community Center. When I first went in and talked to the executive director, I don't think he believed that heart disease was the Number One killer of women. He thought it was a man's disease. I told him my story and he was blown away. So I left him with some information and I said, "Go poll the women that work here and ask them what the Number One killer is." So he did. He asked them if they knew—everyone said breast cancer was the Number One killer. And when he told them my story, their mouths dropped. Suddenly it changed from me talking to a group of ten women, to having a heart health symposium for a thousand women. And that's what happened. It was remarkable.

Reflecting on his long experience as a public advocate—which started when he was a teen—Ocean Robbins is taken by the many places personal stories have led:

I have learned through the years how deeply people respond to authenticity and deep humanity. It resonates and pulls them in. Sometimes, our most painful and traumatic moments carry within them the gift of a deeply moving story that resonates with very deep places in our audience. I knew there must be a way to leverage my family story to bring attention to causes I cherished. In time, I learned that telling my story could also open doorways of contact with people who identified as wealthy and famous, with social justice activists, with parents, grandparents and children. In short, it could be a doorway of connection with almost everyone.

We wish you the best in making a difference in your world and encountering the surprises along the way.

Public Speaking:
Tips and Tools

Delivery Tips

A Collection of Brief Reminders and Guides

Staying Focused

1. Focus the rush of adrenaline. Remember your goal is not to *eliminate* nervous energy, it's to channel it in a productive way. Few things are more dangerous than going into an important public communication without any concern whatsoever.

2. Be realistic. You don't have to be perfect. If something goes wrong, remind yourself of your advocacy goal, why you are here and the positive change for which you advocate.

3. Repeat your advocacy goal to yourself before approaching the speaking area. Remind yourself of why you're here and why you're speaking. Focus on the positive result. Repeat your *Six-Word Reason*.

4. When speaking to a new group, greet or speak to a few audience members beforehand. You'll be guaranteed at least a few smiling faces and positive nonverbal support when you start to speak.

5. Breathe. Public speaking requires breath support. Mindful breathing also calms you and gives the audience time to process what you say. Plan spots in your speech or talk when you will purposefully stop and breathe.

Managing Time

1. Be realistic in what you can achieve. Know your time limits and plan accordingly.

2. Plan for less. If given fifteen minutes, plan for ten. Audience reaction—whether verbal or nonverbal—adds time.

3. Know where your timekeeper is. Decide where you'll look to check your time. Take off your watch and place it on the lectern. Find the clock in the room. Have a colleague give ten- and five-minute signals. Don't worry about hiding the fact that you are mindful of the time.

4. Note your start time. You may have so many things in your head when you begin speaking you may miss the obvious. Jot down your start time so you know how long you have.

5. Use technology. Set the silent vibrating alarm on your cell or smart phone to signal when you're at the five-minute mark. Some presentation software, like Apple's Keynote, have great timers built in. There are also countdown clocks on most smart phones.

Starting Strong

1. Shorten the *run-up*. The *run-up* is the short sprint a high-jumper uses to gain momentum before jumping. It's also the time it takes a speaker to get comfortable in front of an audience. (Watch for it: you can see and hear when a speaker's body and mind relax.) When you begin, think of being the speaker who normally emerges two minutes into your speech. Begin with *that* speaker.

2. Focus on one goal. If you tend to have a quiet voice, make it your goal to start with strong vocal energy. If you have trouble maintaining eye contact, make it your goal to focus on eye contact from the very start.

3. Make your first words strong. The first words out of your mouth are the first words of your presentation. Plan them. If you begin with, "Um, hi. Okay.—" this is how your talk begins. First words, like first impressions, matter—so make them meaningful.

4. Pre-view the audience. If you can, watch the audience before you speak. Position yourself where you can see them. Get a read on the audience's mood.

5. Know your physical approach. If possible, get into the space where you'll speak and practice moving to the speaking area. When you speak, confidently approach the speaking area. If sitting, purposefully sit up.

Using Language

1. Avoid tentative phrases. "I'd like to talk a little bit about—" and "What I hope to show you—" are examples of hesitant language about your topic and story. Used too often, they project a lack of confidence.

2. If everything is important, nothing is. Avoid repetitive phrases such as "most importantly," "basically," "the bottom line is…"

3. **Use signposts.** Giving a presentation is like taking your audience on a journey. Point out what is important and where you're going next: "That's one reason we need this program. Another is…"

4. **Avoid jargon or technical terms.** Your audience may not be as familiar with the world of your story as you are. Be careful of using jargon; if using technical terms, provide definitions or context.

5. **Reduce "verbal filler."** Everyone uses an occasional *um* and *uh*. A few here and there aren't critical. But if frequent, they'll detract from your story and message. Practice inserting silence instead of "ums." With time, you gain control and can "turn them on and off." NOTE: work on this *only* during practice. Don't think about verbal pauses while you're speaking.

Using Your Voice

1. **Vary your speed.** Pausing helps eliminate verbal filler, and will help regulate a fast speaking rate. Vary your speaking rate to emphasize key messages and add interest. Breathe.

2. **Pump up the vocal energy.** You don't need to over-enunciate or be unnaturally animated. But think of using an energy level two notches above the audience. Putting more power behind your voice will aid articulation, volume and expression.

3. **Relax and clear your throat.** Before you speak, practice yawning, take a few long, deep breaths or hum. Drink plenty of water the day you are to speak. Avoid clogging beverages and foods such as

chocolate and milk. If you feel your throat tighten as you speak, pause and simply swallow.

4. Vary the volume. Find the appropriate volume. Can your audience hear you without straining? Or are you so loud the people in the next room can hear you?

5. Articulate clearly. You'll need to be extra crisp, especially if you have an echoing room.

Staging and Presence

1. Look at the people you're talking to. If you scan the audience or look away frequently, you'll appear evasive. Find the individuals in the audience.

2. Make stance and movement purposeful. Eliminate pacing and shifting. Plant both feet squarely beneath you. This will also help you project your voice and gestures more easily. But move when you have a reason to move. Transitions between sections of your talk, or before and after key points in your story, provide perfect opportunities to move. It's also a subtle way to help your audience follow the structure of your presentation.

3. Cross-focus. If you move to the right, look to the audience on the left. If you move to the left, look to the audience on the right.

4. Show you don't need the lectern. One of the most effective ways to use a lectern is to show your listeners you don't need it. Open yourself up to your audience by moving toward them, or stand to the side of the lectern.

5. **If using notes, don't hide.** While your goal is to speak improvisationally, there are times when you may need notes on an index card or a single sheet of paper. Don't try to hide the fact that you have notes, but be aware that they can distract attention. Practice with them. Look for somewhere you can set notes when you don't need them.

Managing Emotions

1. **Breathe.** If you become overcome with the emotion (whether sadness, anger or giddy joyfulness), pause and take a few deep breaths before going on. The audience will appreciate it; they probably could use a breather too.

2. **Return to your purpose.** When you stop to take that breath, remind yourself of what you're doing and why you're doing it—the goals of your advocacy. It's also helpful to do this before you begin speaking as a way to focus.

3. **Reground.** A technique used by performers who find themselves losing attention is to make physical contact with something—the table next to you, a lectern, something in your pocket—and focus on it for just a moment. Because emotions can take us "out of the moment," contact with an object can bring you back. Then breathe and continue.

4. **Name it.** It is sometimes necessary, even helpful, to let the audience know what's going on, that you're taking a moment to compose so you can convey to them your important message.

5. **Return to your positive change.** In the moment you take to gather yourself, recall the positive change your story and advocacy represents, and the better world you envision.

Speaking During Meals

1. **Time it right.** Whenever possible, speak with the hosts or wait staff to find out how the meal will be served. You often can schedule your talk while the least clinking and chewing is taking place.

2. **Change the seating.** Rather than having the audience sit all the way around a round table, ask that places be set only along half of the table so that no one will have to crane a neck or swivel to see you.

3. **Don't compete with the beef.** Delicious food can distract your audience from your speech. Consider shortening what you have to say so they can get to their meals.

4. **Do compete with the beer.** Given the time of day, the size of the meal and whether alcoholic beverages are served, your audience may be a bit drowsy. Recognize that your energy level may need to be punched up a notch, depending on these factors.

5. **Move.** Because there are so many distractions during a meal, and certain seating configuration may not be ideal, consider moving at times while you speak, positioning yourself in various places to make it easier for the audience to see you.

Using Visual Aids

1. **Know why you're using them.** Visual aids are just that: aids. They support your message, accentuate it, make it more memorable. If you're only telling your story, consider whether you really need anything other than your own engaging delivery. Consider the physical space, the size of the room and audience, and sight lines when deciding to use visual aids. Large, projected images are appropriate for a large audience, but may overwhelm a small group.

2. **Be prepared to do without them.** Ultimately, you are the talk, not your visuals. Plan to speak without them and you'll be surprised how few you really need. You'll also be better prepared should anything go wrong with the technology.

3. **Practice.** Incorporating any visual aid—whether it's a slide show, video, a prop or a handout—brings in another technical element to your presentation. Practice with the aid so you can use it smoothly and without distraction.

4. **Maintain control.** Every visual aid should have a purpose. If it doesn't or if it simply repeats what you say, omit it. Edit visual aids mercilessly. Realize that you don't always need to have a visual aid present. Take visuals away if they'll steal focus from what you're saying. Then bring them back as needed.

5. **Avoid pointers.** If you're using visuals, don't assume you need to use a pointer to direct audience attention. Pointers can subordinate your position by planting you off to the side of the screen. They also inhibit your gestures. Instead, try to close the gap between you and any visuals by moving closer to them and gesturing naturally.

Handling Questions from the Audience

A Four-Step Process

Your advocacy situations may occasionally include a question-and-answer session with the audience. Your mission during any Q&A is to answer as many questions as possible, while keeping the group focused on the key messages and your advocacy goal. Unless this session is being moderated by someone else, you may need to facilitate the Q&A yourself. Doing so, your role changes slightly from someone telling a story and delivering key messages to someone now facilitating a discussion. Aim to:

- Clear up any confusion listeners have about your presentation or story.
- Prevent a single question or questioner from dominating the process.
- Draw links (see *Deflecting/Blocking and Bridging*, page 117) between questions or answers and your story or key messages.

While there are no hard-and-fast rules for answering questions, this four-step process can increase the level of control you have over any Q&A session. Eye contact is key.

1. Give focus to the question and the questioner.
- Listen carefully.
- Establish and keep eye contact with the questioner.
- Clarify confusing questions.

2. Pull focus back to the key messages of your presentation and story.

- Repeat or rephrase questions for focus and clarity, and so that everyone can hear.
- Identify issues when questions are controversial or unanswerable.
- Give eye contact to others in the audience (not just the questioner).

3. Answer.

- Keep eye contact on others in the audience (fight your desire to look only at the questioner).
- Be concise. Be honest.
- If you don't have an answer, admit it, but include a next step.
- Don't let the discussion stray into areas of confidential or personal information you've already deemed inappropriate for inclusion.

4. Give focus to another questioner.

- Check back with the original questioner only if you want or need to.
- Remember that your responsibility is to the whole audience, not an individual.

Before the Q&A session begins, let your audience know how much time you have: "We have about fifteen minutes for your questions." Don't end the Q&A session abruptly. Let the audience know: "We have time for two or three more questions." Finally, when you have finished answering questions, repeat the main theme or key messages of your presentation and story, or repeat your call to action. This technique will bring closure to the process and reinforce your advocacy messages.

See *Handling Questions from a Reporter* (page 174) for more suggestions on managing specific types of questions.

Speaking Prep Sheet

Prepare for Your Audience

Demographic Information What ages are represented in the audience? What genders? Religions? Racial, ethnic or cultural backgrounds? Does the audience represent members of a particular group or organization? What is the socio-economic makeup of the audience? Consider language levels, appropriateness of content, culturally significant material, values and beliefs, issues of particular importance and points of difference and similarity between you and the audience.	**Demographic Information**
Situational Information Why has the audience gathered to listen to you? Will the audience be aware of any other news, good or bad, and have it in mind when they hear you speak? Are they under internal or external pressure to listen to you? How large will the audience be? Is the setting formal or informal? Consider how your story relates to the audience's reasons for attending, the moods and attitudes they bring, their openness to listening and physical comfort.	**Situational Information**

Prepare for Your Audience *(continued)*

Attitudes toward Your Topic What do they know about your subject, cause, campaign or organization? What do they need to know about it? What do they want to know about it? What do they expect to hear? What is their level of interest in your subject, cause, campaign or organization? Consider how you frame your story, any background information you may need to cover, what may surprise them, how you "hook" them, how you bring them new information.	**Attitudes toward Your Topic**
Attitudes toward You What is the relationship between you and your audience? What preconceived notions might they have about you? How much do they know about you and your experience? What information have they been given about you and your life experience? Consider how you frame your story, what background information you need to cover, what preconceptions you need to address, where you start your story, your physical relationship to the audience.	**Attitudes toward You**

Download additional Prep Sheets at www.livingproofadvocacy.com

154

Attitudes toward Personal Stories

How open are they to the idea of hearing personal stories?

With what level of disclosure is the audience comfortable?

Does your story go counter to other stories of which this audience is aware, or is your story familiar?

Has this audience experienced something similar to what you will describe?

Consider level of disclosure, how you frame your story *as* a story, what else you may need to include in addition to your story, how they may respond to the content of your story.

Attitudes toward Personal Stories

Values, Beliefs and Decision-making

What is important to this audience? What do they value?

How do they think? Upon what do they base their decisions?

What may they be skeptical about?

What will seem familiar to them? Foreign?

Consider what support you may need in addition to your story, what about your experience speaks to the audience's values, what may challenge their values or beliefs, what analogies you may need to "bridge the gap," how you frame your story.

Values, Beliefs and Decision-making

Speaking Prep Sheet

Prepare for the Context

What is the speaking situation? What is the event or occasion? An informal meeting, outdoor rally, formal fundraiser? What is the ideal outcome of the occasion? What is it about your story that you or the organizers hope it will add to the event? What will the general mood of the situation be? Solemn, energized, tense, supportive, celebratory? Consider how you frame your story appropriately for the context, what you may need to acknowledge or address in addition to telling your story, whether the stories you intend to share are the best for the situation.	**What is the speaking situation?**
What is your role? Are you the primary speaker, or one of many? What are you responsible for conveying? Your experience only and its connection to the topic, or additional background information about the cause, the organization, etc.? How much control do you have over this situation? Is this entirely of your making, or is there someone else determining the shape or agenda? What is your position on the agenda, if there is one? What happens right before you? Right after? Are you being asked to speak in support of particular messages, or is this speech of your own design? Are there any regulatory restrictions on what you can or cannot say? Consider how your story or messages relate to other scheduled speakers, what information organizers may want you to include in your address, what key messages already exist that you need to link to your story.	**What is your role?**

Download additional Prep Sheets at www.livingproofadvocacy.com

Speaking Prep Sheet

Prepare for the Physical Environment

What are the details of speaking in this physical environment? Do you have two minutes or twenty? How much of your story will you be able to share? How formal is the situation? What time of day and where will this occur? Consider how you scale your story for the time constraints, how you dress for the degree of formality.	**What are the details of speaking in this physical environment?**
Mode of Presentation Are there expectations as to how you will speak or from where (at a lectern, through a bullhorn, on a panel, in a circle, from a sofa)? Is the audience seated or standing? In the balcony above you? Surrounding you? What kind of audio/visual equipment will you need or be expected to use? Is a lectern available? Do you have to use it? Do you need a microphone? Can you get a wireless microphone? Are you speaking during a meal? Consider what the setting asks of your physical staging and use of your voice.	**Mode of Presentation**

Prepare for the Physical Environment *(continued)*

Potential Distractions	Potential Distractions
Is the audience's physical comfort (temperature, seating, etc.) adequate?	
Is the lighting appropriate and efficient? Can the audience see both you and your visual aids (if using them)? Can you see the audience? Is the lighting too dramatic, creating distance between you and the audience?	
What will be behind you as you speak? What visual distractions might there be for the audience?	
How are the acoustics? Does your voice echo or is the room "dead"?	
Consider how event organizers might help you address any improvements to the physical environment or how you may need to alter your delivery to accommodate.	

Download additional Prep Sheets at www.livingproofadvocacy.com

Speaking Prep Sheet

Prepare Your Structure

Introduction
- Gain and focus attention
- Establish purpose
- Preview

Body
- Your story, or
- Your story and additional content structured around key messages

Conclusion
- Remind the audience of key messages
- Present them with a call to action

Speaking Prep Sheet

Prepare Your Action Plan

Attention
- Gain and focus attention
- Relate directly to audience

Need
- Make them feel the need
- Tell your story and support it strongly and vividly

Satisfaction
- Provide a solution

Visualization

- Help them see the solution working

Action

- Tell them exactly what they can do

Download additional Prep Sheets at www.livingproofadvocacy.com

Media Interviews:
Tips and Tools

Interview Tips

A Selection of Quick Pointers and Guides

Striking the Correct Tone

1. **Be yourself.** Speak as you do normally. Don't "try on" a new personality for the interview. You can best channel your nervous energy by forgetting about yourself and focusing on the value of your story. Reporters like talking to real people.

2. **Keep the interview focused on your positive change.** You may have to deflect or block a negative impression with a "No, in fact…" or "No, although…," but don't dwell on it. Move on to your story and its message of positive change.

3. **Deliver your story and messages with confidence.** After all, you know more about the story than anyone.

4. **Maintain your poise.** By maintaining your poise even when responding to the most off-the-wall questions, you present yourself as interested, helpful and in control of yourself.

5. **Keep your interview attitude.** Wait until the interview is entirely over before you relax your interview attitude. Wait until the microphone and/or camera is off or the reporter leaves.

Using Language

1. **Make short, simple and specific statements.** When you think you've answered a question adequately, don't feel compelled to keep talking simply because the reporter has a microphone up to your mouth. If you're satisfied with your answer, sit in silence. Rambling may lead you to say the wrong thing.

2. **For edited interviews, pause after complete statements.** When the interview is edited, the reporter and editor will appreciate these breaks.

3. **Never speak off the record.** The reporter is always working, always gathering information, even when the interview is not taking place. Whether the interview hasn't started yet and you're having a cup of coffee and chatting with the reporter, or the interview is over and you're walking with the reporter to the parking lot, avoid off-the-cuff remarks or comments that might be taken out of context or inserted into your story.

4. **Use your vocabulary, not the reporter's.** Avoid repeating negative, inappropriate or incorrect language (deflect or block it when necessary). While conversationally we borrow words and phrases from others all the time, in a media setting you don't want someone else's words to end up being your quote or sound bite.

5. **Manage the paraphrase.** If the reporter paraphrases your answers, make sure not just the gist is correct, but also the wording. If not, correct it.

Looking Good

1. **Gesture comfortably.** Natural body language creates a positive impression. Lean forward in your chair and feel free to use gestures to emphasize and illustrate your story and key messages.

2. **Use color to your advantage.** For television or web interviews, avoid patterns that will distract the viewer; small prints and stripes tend to shimmer and strobe. Solid colors are safe bets. Avoid wearing all black (your head will appear to float) or all white (depending on your skin tone, it may reflect too much light on your face and wash you out).

3. **Look in the mirror three times.** For television or web interviews, make sure your socks are long enough to cover your shins in case you cross your legs and that your skirt looks as great when you sit down as it does when you stand up. Dangling and flashing jewelry is distracting, so keep it at home. Unbutton your suit jacket when sitting, button it when standing.

4. **Be comfortable.** If you're being interviewed outside, dress for the weather. If you're being interviewed in a television studio, realize most studios are kept cool but can get quite warm when the lights are turned on. Mid-weight clothing or layers are comfortable options. If you learn that the piece is airing much later, dress appropriately for that season.

5. **Be clippable.** If you'll wear a microphone, make sure you have something it can clip onto.

Managing Emotions

See *Managing Emotions* in *Public Speaking: Tips and Tools*. The same advice applies to interviews.

Closing Strongly

1. **Make the most of it.** Try to get the last word in (without interrupting), and make it your call to action or summary of key messages.

2. **Make your call to action clear and specific.** Say clearly what you want the target audience to do, when and how.

3. **Include additional resources.** Provide more places readers, listeners or viewers may go for information: websites, phone numbers, locations.

4. **Summarize key messages.** Remember to stress your key messages one more time. This is especially important if the interview has wandered off topic or gone on longer than planned.

5. **Thank the reporter.** Maintain the good relationship you've built.

Interview Formats

Making the Most of the Media

In-Studio Radio Interviews

1. **Create images.** Because sound is the only stimulus for your audience, remember to use the vivid language of lived experience to help your audience hear, visualize and imagine your story. Paint a picture with your words. Bring the people in your story to life.

2. **Sound your best.** The *uhs* and *ums* we use in conversation can make us sound inarticulate when we speak to the media. Replace these annoying sounds with a pause—you'll give the audience time to grasp what you've said and yourself time to decide what to say next. Speak clearly and distinctly using variety in your pace and inflection. Use your normal volume; the sound technician will ensure you can be heard.

3. **Speak to the interviewer.** When a microphone is in front of you, it's tempting to direct your responses to it. Avoid this and speak instead to the interviewer to maintain a sense of real conversation.

4. **Use notes as needed.** Feel free to keep notes in front of you to remind you of key message points, facts, statistics or organizational information. Be aware that the person talking to you can read upside down, and may ask you about something you've written.

5. **Smile.** It sounds odd, but it's absolutely true listeners can tell when someone on the radio is smiling.

Television Interviews

1. **Arrive early.** Take time to get accustomed to the environment. If you can, sit in the seat or stand where you'll be interviewed, and get used to any technicians moving around so you won't be distracted during the interview.

2. **You're always on.** You may be filmed from a variety of angles and shots, from close ups to full-body shots. Because you may not know what type of shot the cameraperson is using, look interested and comfortable even when you're not talking.

3. **For face-to-face interviews, look at the interviewer.** Think of it this way: you are talking with the interviewer, and the audience is simply looking in. Make eye contact with the interviewer as you speak and listen. Strong eye contact keeps you focused and projects confidence to the people watching you. Glancing away or at the camera can make you look evasive or uncomfortable.

4. **Build rapport.** If possible, talk to the interviewer before the on-camera interview so you can get a sense of his or her personality. The interviewer may ask for a thumbnail sketch of your story or let you know how the interview will start. Mention some topics or points you'd like to discuss. Let the interviewer know you want to make this a good interview.

5. **Consider the editor.** Don't overlap questions. Begin your answer when the question is finished. Don't say the reporter's name or

refer to a previous answer or discussion in the middle of a sentence ("as I said earlier, Pete"). This will be difficult to edit.

Face-to-Face Print Interviews

The length of a print interview can vary greatly depending upon the publication and the reporter. For a feature story, it could take an hour or more; for a local daily, just ten minutes or so. Most television tips listed above apply also to print interviews. Here are a few more:

1. **Take your time.** There is no camera on you, no audience waiting for your next word. Just a reporter (on deadline) recording your information. So take your time. After the reporter asks a question, take a moment to gather your thoughts before speaking.

2. **You're always on.** The interview is not over until the interviewer leaves. Don't assume the interview is over just because she or he has closed the notebook.

3. **Be ready to be recorded.** Expect the interview to be audio-recorded (you may be asked to approve this), as it is helpful for the interviewer to quote you accurately.

4. **Use notes as needed.** Feel free to keep notes in front of you, to remind you of key message points, facts and statistics or organizational information. Be ready for the reporter to ask to see them or ask you for a copy.

5. **Look around you.** The reporter is like a camera, making notes of your environment, attitude and reactions for use in the story. If the interview setting is not neutral turf, think about what is

around you and what else the reporter is looking at: framed photographs, notes on the table, poor eye contact. What can you remove, restage or adjust?

Telephone Interviews for Print or Radio

1. **Prepare.** Be ready. You don't want to pick up the phone and find yourself suddenly in an interview. If caught by surprise, say you're busy and make arrangements to call the reporter back at another time. Get the reporter's name, the organization, the topic to be discussed and the deadline. Then prepare: know the target audience, find out about the reporter, practice your story and know your key messages.

2. **Stand up.** By standing, you project your voice and sound more confident. You'll also feel more in control of the interview. However, be careful not to create additional noise or get distracted by something outside your window.

3. **Make your space work for you.** Create a space where you can take the call comfortably and with focus. Get rid of the barking dogs or curious colleagues. Feel free to keep your messages in front of you and have a pen handy to take notes.

4. **Check in.** Check in with the reporter occasionally to make sure you're being understood and heard clearly.

5. **Turn off other technology.** Get rid of anything that might distract: other phones, televisions, email, text or incoming call alerts.

Direct-to-Camera Interviews for Television or Web

If you've watched CNN, you've seen a satellite remote interview: a reporter in Atlanta talking to an expert in Boston. The expert in Boston wears an earpiece and looks directly into a camera and the reporter in Atlanta does the same. Direct-to-camera interviews may be disconcerting at first, because you have no one to look at, just a camera lens, and only the reporter's voice coming to you through an earpiece. It's a slightly surreal setting. Internet-based media takes advantage of your computer's camera and microphone to conduct similar types of interviews between reporters (or bloggers) and guests, both of whom sit in front of their computers and may or may not be able to see each other in separate windows on their desktops.

1. **Treat the camera as a person.** Maintain strong eye contact with the camera's lens just as you would with an actual reporter. If your eyes dart or watch something off-camera, you can appear uncomfortable or distracted.

2. **Be an active listener who's always on.** Use good listening behavior, as you would if you were looking into the face of a reporter. Assume the camera is always on you, from before the interview to several moments after you're confident it has concluded. Consider your facial expressions throughout the interview.

3. **Focus.** When interviewed for the web, focus on your computer's web camera, *not* the face of the reporter in a separate window. Resist looking at other things on your computer screen (including, perhaps, your own image). If necessary, cover what's on your screen so you can focus on the camera.

4. **Present with your whole self.** While you may be recorded from only the shoulders up, continue to move your head naturally to nod or speak. Maintain good posture and gesture naturally. Keep your voice clear and engaged. Part of your interview may cut away to images or graphics, and listeners may only have the sound of your voice to engage them.

5. **Maintain your poise.** If any technical difficulty occurs—if you don't hear the question, for example—maintain your poise and focus on bridging to key messages. "I'm not quite sure I heard your full question because of some interference, but I think it related to one of our key issues."

Handling Questions from a Reporter

Common Queries and Agile Answers

The kind of questions interviewers ask you depend upon many things: their knowledge of your story and cause, their attitude toward your topic, the amount of time they've had to prepare and their level of skill as interviewers. Do your analysis of the situation to prepare for any questions you might get and use the four interview techniques (Deflecting/Blocking, Bridging, Flagging and Headlining) to build your skills in responding to these common types of questions.

Type of Question	For Example	How to Respond
Closed Questions	Straight yes-or-no questions. *"Did you actually see this happen?"* *"The prognosis is really bleak, isn't it?"*	Respond or deflect, then bridge to your story or message: *"I did. And it just underscored for me the importance of..."* *"Advances have been made with treatments and the good news is..."*
Open Questions	An open-ended question that is designed to elicit a full response. *"What happened?"*	Score! Take it where you'd like: go to your story, your headline or your key messages.
Rapid-Fire	Several questions, one after another.	Choose one question and answer it; ignore the rest or return to them later if you'd like. *"You touched on several points. Regarding your second question..."*
Interruption	A question asked before you finish your point that steers you away from your story or message and on to another question.	Be polite. Acknowledge the question, but return to and finish the story moment or point you were making.

Type of Question	For Example	How to Respond
Darts	Negative questions that challenge: *"How could you have been so irresponsible?*	Refocus the question: *"That's not it at all. Like many others, I was ill-informed ..."* Avoid using the negative language yourself.
Vague	Often from an underprepared reporter, these questions require you to provide a lot of background before you can get to your key message.	Score! Steer the interview in the direction you want it to go. Rephrase the question to make it more specific. *"By your question, I think you're referring to the damage this kind of pollution can cause..."*
Off-topic	Irrelevant or tangential question that leads you and the interview off track.	Deflect/block and bridge. *"That's interesting. At tomorrow's rally, though, we'll be focusing on..."*
Loaded Preface	A question that starts with negative or incorrect information. *"As an organization for women with ovarian cancer, what kinds of programs are available at Gilda's Club?"*	Correct the incorrect information in a positive way. *"The great thing about Gilda's Club is that it's for anyone dealing with any type of cancer: men, women, friends, family. And the programs are..."*
Impossible	A question you do not know the answer to.	Acknowledge that you cannot answer it and why. Offer to find the answer, if possible. *"I'm not a scientist, so I can't answer that question, though I know someone at the Center who could. But what I can tell you is..."*
Gut-Punch	A question designed to engage your emotions. *"Can you tell me what it felt like when you first got the news of his death?"*	Look to your emotional preparation and what you feel you can safely and honestly say while maintaining focus on your goal. Answer and bridge, or deflect and bridge: *"It felt like my world had ended. But of course it didn't. So, two months later..."* *"It was really hard, but what I now realize is..."*

Interview Prep Sheet

Prepare for Your Audience

Demographic Information What ages are represented in the target audience? What genders? Religions? Racial, ethnic or cultural backgrounds? Does the target audience represent members of a particular group or organization? What is the socio-economic makeup of the target audience? Consider language levels, appropriateness of content, culturally significant material, values or beliefs of a certain demographic, issues of particular importance to them and points of difference and similarity between you and the audience.	**Demographic Information**
Situational Information Why has the audience tuned in or picked up the magazine? Are they passionately attentive or multi-tasking? If broadcast, will the audience be aware of any other news, good or bad, and have it in mind when they hear you speak? What are the specialties or concerns of the media publication or program? What is the focus or angle of the media interview or story? What led to this interview or appearance? Consider how your story relates to the audience's reasons for listening to you, the moods and attitudes they bring, their openness to listening.	**Situational Information**

Download additional Prep Sheets at www.livingproofadvocacy.com

Attitudes toward Your Topic

What do they know about your subject, cause, campaign or organization?

What do they need to know?

What do they want to know?

What do they expect to hear?

What is their level of interest?

Consider how you frame your story, any background information you may need to cover, what may surprise them, how you "hook" them, how you bring them new information.

Attitudes toward Your Topic

Attitudes toward You

What preconceived notions might they have about you?

How much do they know about you and your experience?

What information have they been given about you and your life experience?

Consider how you frame your story, what background information you need to cover, what preconceptions you need to address, where you start your story.

Attitudes toward You

Attitudes toward Personal Stories

How open are they to the idea of hearing personal stories?

With what level of disclosure is the audience comfortable?

Does your story go counter to other stories of which this audience is aware or is your story familiar?

Has this audience experienced something similar to what you will describe?

Consider level of disclosure, how you frame your story *as* a story, what else you may need to include in addition to your story, how they may respond to the content of your story.

Attitudes toward Personal Stories

Prepare for Your Audience *(continued)*

Values, Beliefs and Decision-making	Values, Beliefs and Decision-making
What is important to this audience? What do they value?	
How do they think? Upon what do they base their decisions?	
What may they be skeptical about?	
What will seem familiar to them? Foreign?	
Consider what support you may need in addition to your story, what about your experience speaks to the audience's values, what may challenge their values or beliefs, what analogies you may need to "bridge the gap," how you frame your story.	

Download additional Prep Sheets at www.livingproofadvocacy.com

Interview Prep Sheet

Prepare for the Context

What is the media situation? What is the reason for the interview? Why are you being interviewed at this time? Is it in response to other news, the time of year, a controversy arising, an upcoming event or general interest? What is the focus or angle of this story? Are there other people the interviewer may have spoken to for the story? What kind of deadline is the interviewer under? Consider how your subject or story relates to the target audience's interest in and reasons for listening to you, whether there may be questions regarding others news or events, what the best version of your story is to tell.	**What is the media situation?**
Your Role Are you the sole interviewee or one of many? What do you want to convey? Your story only or background information about the cause or the organization? Prepare the specific key messages you need to convey in the interview and practice any additional information for which you may be responsible; research other potential interviewees.	**Your Role**

Download additional Prep Sheets at www.livingproofadvocacy.com

Prepare for the Context *(continued)*

What are the details of the interview? How long will the interview be? Is it TV or radio broadcast, online, print newspaper or magazine? Is it live or taped, edited or unedited? In studio, on location, sitting or standing? Telephone? Via the Internet? Are there expectations in terms of the degree of formality or what you are to wear? Practice fitting your story and messages to the appropriate time frame, look to *Interview Formats* (page 168) for help with particular media forms.	**What are the details of the interview?**
The Interviewer How familiar is the reporter with your cause? Does she or he have preconceived ideas or biases? Based on what you've seen, heard or read of the interviewer's other work, what type of questions does he or she ask? Does the interviewer seem prepared? New to the job or seasoned? What tone can you expect from this interviewer in terms of his or her support of your cause? Write and practice answering questions you might expect from this interviewer; know the first message or headline you want to stress and what call to action you want to end with.	**The Interviewer**

Download additional Prep Sheets at www.livingproofadvocacy.com

Index

References

For more information about the advocates in *Living Proof*, and to access additional resources for telling your story, visit www.livingproofadvocacy.com

Alva, Eric. "Don't Ask, Don't Tell: Telling My Story to Congress." *The HuffingtonPost.com*. The Huffington Post, Inc., 23 July 2008. Web. 10 Mar. 2010.

Carter, Majora. "Greening the Ghetto." *TedTALKS*. TED Conferences, LLC, 27 June 2006. Web. 10 Mar. 2010.

Dale, Gregory. "Nonprofit Organization Makes Music 'Pop' for Students." Summer 2010, Trends. Baltimore: Afro-American Newspapers. *soulpopuniversity.com*. Web. 7 Nov. 2011

Fershleiser, Rachel and Larry Smith, eds. *Not Quite What I Was Planning: Six-Word Memoirs by Writers Famous and Obscure*. New York: Harper, 2008. Print.

Genette, Girard. *Narrative Discourse: An Essay in Method*. Ithaca: Cornell UP, 1980. Print.

Harrison, Scott. "The story of charity: water by founder Scott Harrison." *charity: water.org*. charity: water, 21 Sept. 2010. Web. 10 Mar. 2010.

Jackson, Shirley. *Come Along With Me*. New York: Penguin Books, 1995. Print.

Kastan, Kathy. *From the Heart: A Woman's Guide to Living Well with Heart Disease*. Cambridge: Perseus Book Group, 2007. Print.

Loeb, Paul Rogat. *Soul of a Citizen: Living with Conviction in Challenging Times*. New York: St. Martin's Griffin, 2010. Print.

Lucas, Stephen E. *The Art of Public Speaking*. New York: McGraw Hill, 2012. Print.

Maguire, Jack. *The Power of Personal Storytelling*. New York: Jeremy Tarcher & Putnam, 1998. Print.

McKee, Robert. *Story: Substance, Structure, Style and the Principles of Screenwriting*. New York: HarperCollins, 1997. Print.

Radner, Gilda. *It's Always Something*. New York: HarperCollins, 1989. Print.

Rainer, Tristine. *Your Life as Story*. New York: Jeremy Tarcher & Putnam, 1998. Print.

"Read Others' Stories." National Meningitis Association, 2010. Web. 24 Sept. 2011.

Robbins, Ocean. "Opening Keynote, National Alliance for Peace, Washington, DC." *Oceanrobbins.com*. Ocean Robbins, 2009. Web. 10 Mar. 2010.

Schank, Roger C. *Tell Me a Story: Narrative and Intelligence.* Evanston: Northwestern University Press, 1995. Print.

Spry, Tami. *Body, Paper, Stage: Writing and Performing Autoethnography.* Walnut Creek: Left Coast Press, 2011. Print.

"To Increase Charitable Donations, Appeal to the Heart – Not the Head." *Knowledge@Wharton.* University of Pennsylvania, 27 June 2007. Web. 24 Sept. 2011.

Turner, Victor. *The Anthropology of Performance.* New York: PAJ Publications, 1986. Print.

Vaillancourt, Loren. "Beauty queen takes on distracted driving." *CBSNews.com.* CBS News, 7 Mar. 2010. Web. 10 Mar. 2010.

Whybrow, Helen, ed. *The Story Handbook: A Primer on Language and Storytelling for Land Conservationists.* White River Jct.: Chelsea Green Publishing, 2003. Print.

Acknowledgments

W
e wouldn't be doing the work we do—let alone be writing this book—had we not paid attention to mentors and colleagues Beverly Long Chapin, Martha Nell Hardy, Dennis Beagen, Annette Martin, Ron Pelias and Jim Van Oosting. Thanks to Mr. Ries and Ms. Seegers (Richard and Deborah Lee) for teaching generations of junior high and high school students to be passionate about communication.

An amazingly talented community of storytellers and writers contributed insight and advice, especially Irene Ziegler, Cathy Camper, Joanne Gilbert, Robrt Pela and Rachael Quitta. Tami Spry and Cindy Meier provided smart, supportive and poetic words when they were needed most. Our network of advisors was extended greatly thanks to Maureen Burke, Renee Holoien, Holly Morris and Dana Wilde. The expertise of fellow trainers and educators echoes throughout *Living Proof*; thanks to Poppy Gaskin, Dale Ludwig, Eddah Mutua-Kombo, Elyse Pineau, Lisa Samra and especially Jeff Bloch and Gail Quattlebaum for pointing the way down such rewarding paths.

We're honored and privileged to have heard the stories of so many inspirational advocates over so many years and are particularly grateful to those who generously contributed their stories to this book: Becky Blanton, Derek Cotton, Glenton Davis, Theresa Greenleaf, Kathy Kastan, Ocean Robbins and Loren Vaillancourt. We are also grateful to many others who gave their time in interviews. The following organizations contributed great examples of story advocacy:

charity: water, Gilda's Club Twin Cities, WomenHeart: The National Coalition for Women with Heart Disease and the National Meningitis Association.

This book would never have made it out of our heads were it not for a crack support team: coach Linda Strommer, first editor Laurie Walker and reviewers David Cohen, Sonja Foss, Loretta Kane, Nancy Loving, Gordon Mayer, Susan Raffo and Leslie Shore. Very special thanks to Bev Bachel for sharp, substantive edits, for sharing her considerable knowledge of all things bookish and writerly, for enthusiastic pep talks and invaluable connections.

Finally, thanks to our dear cast of friends and family members who help us write the stories of our lives everyday, and to Rob Kirby and Eric Nelson, the main characters.

About the Authors

Authors **John Capecci** and **Timothy Cage** have helped thousands of advocates and hundreds of organizations share their stories in compelling and engaging ways in order to increase awareness, educate or raise money.

Since meeting as classmates more than twenty years ago in a graduate school course about bringing stories to life, John and Tim have worked with a wide range of clients, from "ordinary" people and first-time speakers, to CEOs and entrepreneurs, and some of the best-known celebrities, media personalities and professional speakers in the world. Their clients are business professionals, educators, nonprofit leaders, marketing/PR agencies and everyday advocates working in the arts, healthcare and wellness, manufacturing, financial, consumer marketing, travel, design and high-tech industries.

John Capecci is a communication trainer and educator who has published and spoken on the use of narrative to educate and persuade. He's co-editor of a best-selling series of monologue anthologies, *Sixty Seconds to Shine,* and owner of Capecci Communications (www.capeccicom.com), a firm he founded in 1998. Prior to this, he taught public speaking, communication theory, interpretation of literature and advanced performance courses at Eastern Michigan University. He received his Ph.D. in speech communication from Southern Illinois University and an M.A. in communication studies from The University of North Carolina at Chapel Hill. John currently serves on the advisory board for The Soap Factory, a visual arts organization in Minneapolis, volunteers with other local nonprofits and works to preserve his historic neighborhood along the banks of the Mississippi.

Tim Cage conducts media and presentation skills workshops and seminars for the highest levels of senior management, and with all manner of spokespersons. He launched Timothy Cage Communication Training (www.timothycage.com) in 1993. Previously, Tim was vice president and training manager for Burson-Marsteller, a worldwide PR/public affairs agency, in charge of counseling chief executive officers and spokespersons. Prior to that, Tim was senior associate at an international communications skills training company, consulting with politicians and business executives. He graduated from the University of Illinois with a B.S. in marketing and from The University of North Carolina at Chapel Hill with an M.A. in communication studies. Tim lectures on public relations and business communication at New York University, and has taught oral communication and interpersonal behavior courses for Cornell University's Industrial and Labor Relations Cooperative Extension Program. Tim is a founding member and former chairman of The University of North Carolina's Department of Communication Studies Advisory Board. He also serves on the board of directors for Bach Vespers at Holy Trinity in New York City and is the board's past president.

Living Proof Advocacy Training[SM]

John Capecci and Tim Cage offer individual, small-group
or multi-trainer sessions, customized to meet your
specific needs, including

- **Presentation Skill Development**
- **Media Interview Training and Preparation**
- **Personal Story Training for Advocates and
  Spokespersons**

The authors are available to speak on the subject of
personal narratives and advocacy.

For information, contact **info@livingproofadvocacy.com**

Visit us at **www.livingproofadvocacy.com**
Befriend us on Facebook—**LivingProof.TellingYourStory**
Follow us on Twitter **@livproof**